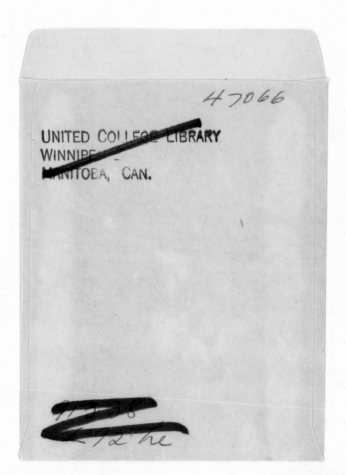

HELLAS AND ROME

W. ZSCHIETZSCHMANN

HELLAS AND ROME

The Classical World in Pictures

UNIVERSE BOOKS, PUBLISHERS, NEW YORK

The illustration on the cover shows the columns of the temple at Corinth and is from a photograph by Martin Huerlimann

First American Edition
published in the United States of America in 1960 by
UNIVERSE BOOKS, Inc.
381 Park Avenue South
New York 16, New York
translated by Hedi Schnabl
Library of Congress Catalog Card Number 60-8173
© Verlag Ernst Wasmuth, 1959

Printed in Germany

CONTENTS

ACKNOWLEDGEMENTS

The publishers wish to thank the following institutes, firms and private persons for permission to reproduce photographs in their possession:

Albertina, Dresden 4 photos · Alinari, Florence 14 photos · Anderson, Rome 8 photos · Antikensammlung, Munich 5 photos · Deutsches Archäologisches Institut, Athens 8 photos · Deutsches Archäologisches Institut, Rome 82 photos · Archäologisches Institut der Universität Tübingen 24 photos · British Museum, London 1 photo · Hirmer, Munich 8 photos · Foto Marburg, Marburg 35 photos · The Metropolitan Museum of Art, New York 7 photos · Staatliche Kunstsammlungen, Kassel 1 photo · Staatliche Museen, Berlin 71 photos · Zentral-Bildarchiv, Giessen 5 photos · Bettermann, Giessen 1 photo · W. Braun-Elwert, Marburg 5 photos · E. M. Czako, Athens 1 photo · Gärtner, Giessen 3 photos · H. Hell, Reutlingen 2 photos · A. Kerber, Frankfurt 1 photo · E. Langlotz, Bonn 1 photo · B. von Tiesenhausen, Giessen 5 photos · G. Wehrheim 3 photos.

32 illustrations are taken from volumes of the Corpus Vasorum, 41 from the publisher's archives and the rest from those of the author.

Anyone who studies the classical age or attempts to gain some insight into it will inevitably read the literary heritage of this period in Greek or Latin, thus becoming familiar with the poets and philosophers. But no one can overlook the fact that beside the written word, indeed beyond it, there exists in painting and sculpture a more direct and vivid way of gaining a vision of the details of everyday life, with its customs and manners, in both its public and private aspects. Indeed an insight into the entire classical culture is provided by the world of plastic art created by the Greeks and Romans. The works of poets, statesmen, philosophers and orators must necessarily be translated and interpreted whereas pictures provide a direct means of communication, but their greatest value lies in the fact that they not only portray an aspect of classical life but also form a part of that life and thus represent a considerable portion of its culture.

These pictures are therefore not merely a welcome illustration of literary documents, giving the written word a new emphasis, but are also integral with the literature of the period, the one complementing the other. How far could the imagery of ancient mythology, in particular Greek mythology, be comprehended by merely reading Homer or the playwrights without looking at pictures? What Greek poet has created so definite an image of Apollo as is depicted in the representation of this god on the West Pediment of the Temple of Zeus at Olympia? What Greek author of the so-called Hellenistic period (3rd – 1st cent. B.C.) was as interested in the description of life among the lower classes as was plastic art? Roman writers produced pictorial descriptions of individuals because the art of biography was widespread and popular; but what author can describe the animation of the human soul as deftly as it is done in plastic representations? A survey of the gallery of Roman portraits from the end of the Republic until the late Roman period shows hardly any human trait which has not been honestly, truthfully, even ruthlessly represented. There can be seen humor beside vanity, insensitivity next to sensitivity, lust and vice, discipline and laxity, brute force and noble sacrifice, cunning, treachery, depravity and the touching melancholy of a childlike decadence. All this is tangible, direct and readily perceived because it is placed before the spectator by means of plastic art.

Examples such as these give some indication of the importance of classical art and show how pictures are one of the primary sources for our knowledge of antiquity, a fact that is often overlooked. Not one single work of classical art, neither the most important nor the most insignificant, was created for its own sake alone. All the monuments reproduced on the following pages had a definite purpose within the life they represented and they were created for that purpose. Today we tend to admire merely the work of art forgetting thereby its function. The reason for this is to be found in the isolation of the individual examples in different museums where they are severed from their true environment. The notes give some indication of this.

Plastic art has been chosen here as a way of entering the world of antiquity because its appeal is the most direct. The plastic heritage of classical times is vast – it would be possible to collect a great variety of pictures to illustrate the subjects chosen for the plates without in any way exhausting all those available.

HELLAS AND ROME shows how classical culture is a definitive unity, how it can be separated on the one hand in time and style from the civilization of earlier times in the Mediterranean area and the Near East, and on the other hand how it can be separated from the culture of Christianity which had grown up during the same period within the territory of classical civilization. Every expert knows and every attentive reader of this book will recognize the difference between the Greek and the Roman mind. If the beginning of the period is compared with the end it will seem inconceivable that they should be related. They do, however, merge into one living unit when the historical events which represent the destinies of both nations are considered.

The centuries following the Greek classical period have been termed the Hellenistic period because during this time events took place which were spread over a long period of time and a vast area of land reaching to the furthest corner of Mediterranean cultures. This process demonstrates clearly the unity of classical civilization for it unified the people who came under the same cultural influence and formed them into one Mediterranean people. It was a process of spreading Greek culture to peoples originally untouched by it. The Romans more than any others came under the influence of Greek culture and that is why they in their turn were able to pass it on to the rest of the Europe which developed from the unique civilization of classical times.

DEITIES

Pages 1-25

The gods governed the lives of the Greeks as well as of the Romans at all times. Religion permeated every aspect of their culture. Private as well as public demeanor was based on religion: the gods were entreated to protect everyday events. Weddings and funerals carried the stamp of religious celebrations; no Greek would have dared speak in the Symposium without first making an offering of wine to the gods. When the ancients spoke of love, they spoke of Eros or Amor, of Aphrodite or Venus, and they used these names not as abstract conceptions, but referred to them as living deities and real forces. There was no valid abstract "right;" it was left to Themis to judge.

Ares or Mars personally led the wars. Nike or Victory did not mean victory, but goddess of victory, because she herself brought about the victory. Every market place had a temple and altar dedicated to Zeus, Hermes or Apollo; there was no Bouleuterion (the conference room for communal deputations), no Prytaneum (town hall) without a hearth or sacrificial altar, and every single spring was thought to be the dwelling place of nymphs. All great philosophies, the invention of technical apparatus and musical instruments, and even the knowledge of sickness and healing were thought to be of godly origin. "Athena Fashions a Horse" (page 188) means that it is the goddess who fashions the work for the potter and for the brass founder. "Asclepius healing a Sick Woman" (page 285): it is the god himself who appears in the picture, not as a personification of healing but as a living presence, the healer himself.

On the great fast days, when the doors of the Parthenon opened to reveal the marble inner temple of Pallas Athena, glowing with gold and ivory, there appeared to the priests and crowds of believers, not an image of the goddess, but the goddess herself. The chapels and temples which served the cult of the Roman emperors also contained images of the deified imperial Augustus, god of the incarnation of the idea of the Roman empire, of government, and of imperialism. Certainly these august deities were not approached with such personal problems and with such human warmth as the Athenians approached Athena, the Argives Hera, or the simple woman from Brauron Artemis, the deliverer in the hours of travail. The cult of the rulers was more cold and representative in character – but even here the emperor himself served as a living and more personal god. The Romans too believed in the gods, knew that their lives were directed and determined by them, and lived and experienced their religion like all other ancient religious civilizations. Certainly the Roman gods are different from those of the Greeks, even if they appear to correspond; sometimes it seems to us, as though they were less hot-blooded and less "human" than the Greek gods, more intellectual than real. But here appearances may lie and the knowledge we have may deceive us, because the thick labyrinth of complicated rules and regulations and the strict order may blur our vision of the living substance and the real religious life. But all the many sacrificial rules and other precise instructions would not have arisen and been perfected if the being and ruling of the Roman gods had not fulfilled the lives of the people.

1. Zeus has enticed the boy Ganymede, son of the Trojan King Tros, with a cockerel. Now he carries him lovingly in his arms away to Olympus where he will serve as cupbearer to the gods. The

group was once the center acroterium (compare No. 87) of a still unknown building in Olympia, probably the work of a Corinthian workshop.

2. Zeus throws lightning from his right arm – victory and strength for the faithful, annihilation for the enemy – an old motif in early classical form. Some opinions believe it to be Poseidon. (Compare 5, 190, 194). Masterpiece by someone unknown (Kalamis?)

3. Hera sat on the throne and next to her stood Zeus, so-called Pausanias. From a Laconic workshop, remains of the original paint can still be seen on the eyes.

4. Around Apollo rages the battle of the Lapiths against the Centaurs, who, having invited themselves to the wedding of the king, have become intoxicated and are ravishing the young maidens and boys. Apollo, stern and unbending, rules and gives judgment – a marvelous epiphany of the god. In battles like these, the Greeks saw a mythical likeness to their own battles against brutality and barbarism, as well as to their differences with the native population. The temple of Zeus was consecrated in 456 B.C. Compare page 29.

5. Hyacinthus, the beautiful young son of the Spartan king and favorite of Apollo, was killed by a quoit thrown by the god in the sanctuary of Amyclae, where religious homage was paid to him. From his blood grew the lovely flower of the same name. The garlanded boy rides on a flying swan over the sea, which is indicated by waves and dolphins.

6. Artemis, the goddess of animals, is also the goddess of hunting, and she herself slew the deer in the mountains. The small animal, which can be seen next to the great goddess, has been injured by a spear and has collapsed on the rocky slope. The goddess seizes his antlers and deals the deathblow. The folds of her garment show the speed of the movement.

7. The younger Athena in a Peplos and without Aegis (as she was generally presented in the time after the Persian wars, 480 B.C.), is in a casual posture reading the inscription on a stone (boundary stone?). This is the work of an Attic master, one of the group surrounding Myron. Its mood is tender but "a mourning woman" is certainly not depicted.

8. Theseus has just killed the Minotaur. Steps and pillar indicate the labyrinth of the palace of Knossos. Compare the "ornamental stripe" on the right. Athena helped him in his deed, by which he freed Athens for all time from paying tribute to Crete. She stands quietly, armed with a spear and wearing her helmet. On her breast is the Aegis, worn here like a jacket and fastened together by Gorgons in the form of a brooch. (Athena on pages 44, 134, 151, 188, 190, 200, Gorgons page 87). Below: Nike, the goddess of Victory, richly dressed in chiton and jacket, is flying by with wide open wings. In her right hand she carries a helmet (Corinthian), in her left a round shield with a snake as an emblem. The bringing of the arms proclaims Victory.

9. The figure above once stood as the central Acroterium (compare page 87) over the entrance to a hall of pillars in the Agora (State market) of Athens. The chiastic, lively movement of the figure indicates it to be the goddess of Victory and is typical of the style of the time. She is hurrying forward with the emblems of Victory in her hand and glancing back as though looking for followers to carry onwards with her to Victory. The Nike of Paionios on the other hand, floats down from heaven bringing a palm branch as the symbol of Victory. Below her feet, an eagle, the messenger of Zeus, flies past. Dedicated by Naupactus for a Victory over Sparta 421, B.C. The original wings from both works are missing. Compare page 190, 144. (Victoria).

10. Hermes, messenger of the gods, is ordered by Zeus, to take the newly born Dionysus to the nymphs at Nisa to feed and rear him. He is carrying the baby on his arm and holding up a grape (?), which the child is eagerly trying to grasp. This work was done by Praxiteles for the inner sanctum of the temple of Hera. It is an original, and not a copy of later times, as has been maintained.

X

11.   The hat (compare page 23, 185) indicates the messenger of the gods. Hermes earnestly and thoughtfully inclines his head to make a speech, apparently about exalted rights. The work has been attributed both to Pheidias and Myron.

12.   Demeter, the great goddess of Eleusis, carries a scepter. She gives the boy Triptolemus the corn, which he, each year, distributes to the inhabitants of the earth. Core, her daughter (Persephone), is carrying a torch and crowning the youth. Festive severity is here treated in a relaxed style. The figures are larger than life. (If this large relief served as devotion in Eleusis, it would be the only known example, for the Greeks only used three-dimensional figures in their religion).

13.   Triptolemus, the king's son from Eleusis and nursling of Demeter, has mounted the winged dragon chariot which will carry him to the inhabitants of the earth. Every year he brings them the fruit of the harvest and teaches them to serve Demeter.

14.   Dionysus leads Hephaestus back to Olympus to free his mother Hera from the bonds with which he has tied her to her throne; Hephaestus, the god and patron of all artists who work in metal, carries his tools: hammer and tongs (compare page 190). A Satyr from the retinue of Dionysus helps the drunk and the lame. Dionysus himself is bearded. He wears a panther skin over his long clothes. He carries a thyrsus staff and a cup of wine. He walks at the head of the procession, fully aware of the power of his eye and of his wine. This work is by the Cleophon painter and is one of his most beautiful. Continuation: page 260, compare Hephaestus page 190, 191.

15.   Dionysus, the lord of wine, of drunkenness, and of ecstasy, with the symbols of his greatness and power: a garland of ivy in his hair, a long beard, and a lock of hair on his chest, dressed in a flowing robe (Chiton), covered by a large mantle, and carrying the thyrsus staff (a natural branch of pine with cones, or a bunch of ivy leaves like the one the Maenad standing next to him is holding in both hands). Dionysus is always followed by drunkenness and by the noisy madness of his companions, "the frenzied ones" (Maenads). The one seen here with her head thrown back is singing and dancing ecstatically. The work is part of a masterpiece by the Cleophrades painter about 500 B.C. (from the same vessel page 242, other Maenads page 242, 257, 259, 260).

16.   Aphrodite assisted by helpers rises from an abyss. Her wavy hair falls richly at the nape of the neck and a soft strand lies on her right breast. The relief is of exceptional delicacy, the composition is artistic and well thought out, the expression still and restrained. It is the work of an important early Greek master about 470 B.C. Compare the opposite page.

17.   Since the year 400 B.C. Aphrodite, who rose from the sea, is often represented in her bath, as well as before or after it, in accordance with Homer, who described in detail her toilet preparations before meeting her lover Anchises. The large terra cotta figure is beginning to disrobe; the one crouching in the bath is completely naked; the figure reveals the ripe body and youthful face of the goddess. It is said that with this work the master Doidalsas surpassed the Aphrodite of Cnidus by Praxiteles, who was the first to picture the goddess naked.

18.   Since the song of Demodokus in the sixth book of the Odyssey, the Greeks and Romans have always seen the God of War and the Goddess of Love (Ares and Aphrodite, Mars and Venus) in close tender harmony. The God of War has removed his shield and helmet, helped by Eros at his side, before embracing the goddess. Compare Mars page 54.

19.   Above: Eros is the son of the Goddess of Love and, according to Plato, the oldest of the gods. Small winged creatures like him (an early development) accompany the goddess herself and also, especially since 500 B.C., the lives of women. Often they do their work, which is leading people to love, without Aphrodite.

Below: Pluto, with scepter and garland, a horn of plenty in his left hand, stands facing Persephone, Goddess of the Underworld and daughter of Demeter (compare No. 12). She hands him a drinking cup. The horn of plenty is brimming over with fruit, it has the shape of a bull's horn. This is the work of the Dionocles painter.

20. The Goddess of Night, with a cloak over her head, beautiful face and rich hair, slings a vessel entwined with snakes towards a Giant. The battle of the Giants against the Olympic Gods was presented in greatest detail on the outer frieze of the great altar of Pergamum. The baroque motif of the work is unmistakable.

21. With the expressive pathos of Hellenistic Art on his face, Poseidon, the Lord of the Sea, larger than life, stands imperiously gazing into the distance. Compare page 204, Neptune. His left hand is on his hip, and in the other he holds the Trident which Hephaestus has made for him.

22. Above: In the early sixth century B.C. the monster Typhon was seen as a strange creature made up of three snakes which had swallowed each other, and three male trunks. Later, as a sign of his transmutability, he carried fire, water, and air (a bird) in his hand. Typhon, from the right pediment, watched the battle of Hercules against the fish-bodied Triton, which was on the left pediment.

Below: In imagination and presentation, the great Pan has never been completely likened to the human form. Goat's hooves and horned face, and a fur-covered but otherwise human body, mark his appearance. He is sitting on a rock looking at us thoughtfully, with his hand under his beard supporting his chin, and his short legs comfortably crossed.

23. Selene has mounted her two wheeled chariot, and is steering the winged pair of horses across the sea with a thorny stick for a whip. Hermes goes before the horses, there is a new moon and a star; it is a nocturnal journey.

24. Like Helius, the Roman god Sol rises out of the sea with his team of horses. Lights radiate from his youthful head. In front of him can be seen the upper edge of the chariot and the horses. Roman busts of arms were often ornamented with reliefs. Compare page 116.

25. Mithras, the original God of Light of old Persia, killing the bull singlehanded, and looking towards heaven. During the time of the early emperors, the cult of Mithras spread quickly through the whole empire (except Greece) – in Ostia alone there were twenty places of worship.

SANCTUARIES AND CULTS

Pages 26–56

Sanctuaries are consecrated precincts which serve the cults of the gods. There are some differences between Greek and Roman sanctuaries, but they have one thing in common – every sanctuary presents a place cut off and protected from the profane world outside by a stone wall. The height and thickness of the wall, the architectural structure and design, are not important – the only relevant thing is the wall itself, which contains just one door and otherwise debars direct approach. So, an ancient sanctuary is a precinct open to the sky, frequently a holy grove with consecrated trees, as Homer described it, and as it has been discovered in Olympia. This is in direct antithesis to the Christian religion, where all worship and prayer are united under one roof in chapels, churches, or cathedrals, which are closed, vaulted, covered buildings. This "turning towards the inside" was already taking effect before Christianity reached the dominant position it has held since Constantine, under whom it became the state religion. The Pantheon in Rome serves as a good example, because the religiously functional parts of the building are inside. But the followers of a sectarian religion, who held their feasts and meetings in the basilica in front of the Porta Maggiore (page 42), also preferred – we don't know why – the covered inner room, and later the followers of the Mithras cult did the same. Apart from the grotto sanctuaries, in which Pan and the Nymphs were worshipped – natural grottos in rock formations – one exception is known to the rule, namely the Telesterion in Eleusis (page 34); boundary wall, propylaea, temple, altar, holy way – all these are usually part of an ancient sanctuary, but to Eleusis was added a covered room, which was used as an assembly room for the faithful, for the observance of ritual, and in this case for mystic festivals. It is a hall with many naves: the Telesterion. The Propylaeum (gateway) receives the faithful and transforms the road leading up to it into a holy way. This holy way leads from the gateway and the halls behind it to the consecrated places, past the oblations which border its edges, to the great sacrificial altar, the religious centerpiece of the cult. The position of altars in Greek sanctuaries was arbitrary and uninfluenced by discernible architectural laws, for the Greek precincts grew and developed, whereas the Roman ones were planned and built as entities. That is why the Romans used the axial and symmetric laws of architecture to greater advantage, and it becomes clear that isolated parts of a Roman sanctuary mean so little by themselves because they are a part of a whole.

On entering a Roman sanctuary the whole layout could generally be seen at a glance, the path to the altar and to the raised temple at the end; but on entering a Greek sanctuary a great many single points of interest would meet the eye: the holy way, oblations, the altar, halls, and, above all, one or another temple (in a precinct dedicated to one god there was also room for other gods, who therefore had their own temples). The temples, which were the main buildings of a sanctuary, were generally built cornerwise, so that their length and breadth could be seen at the same time, thus showing them to have space and not just facades. An ancient temple was not the meeting place of a faithful community. The congregation stayed outside, grouped around the altar where the religious rites began. The temple was a monumental building, a great shrine for the image inside. The Greeks called a building Naos, which means a dwelling; the temple was the dwelling place of a god. For the ancients an image did not mean a likeness, for the god himself was present in the image. The temple was surrounded by oblations, they overflowed into the entrance hall and stood between the pillars and the outer chambers. Oblations are thanksgiving offerings from individuals, from families, groups, associations, from towns and states, offerings to the deities in gratitude for their help. So many reasons for the offerings, and so many different kinds of offerings: sashes (page 43), painted wood or terra cotta tablets (page 188), inscriptions, single figures or groups of figures – nearly all of the many sculptures of ancient times can be traced back as offerings. It is probable that the Greek sanctuaries became great open-air museums as time went by, and before they were publicly and privately plundered by the Romans, for although the Greeks had no classified museums or exhibitions as we know them, the common purpose of the oblations gave them a unity. Precious objects were guarded by the town in special houses built for them, and which were called Thesauroi (treasure houses). These houses were generally placed along the holy way, as in Delphi (page 32).

26. The Acropolis in Athens was a citadel and stronghold in older times, and became a holy precinct only since classical times. It is the central place of worship of Athena, also called Parthenos,

the virgin Goddess of the City. She is lying on a high rock, as though it were a natural pedestal. The Parthenon dominates everything. On the southern slope there were other precincts, one with a theater belonging to Dionysus (page 58), and one consecrated to Asclepius. In the background is the great sanctuary of Zeus Olympius, called the Olympium (page 84).

27. The picture shows the building which Pericles had erected by the master builders Iktinos and Kallikrates after the year 448 B.C. It is seen as the visitor saw it when he crossed the Propylaea. Seventeen pillars along one side and eight along the other form a Peristasis around the Cella, in which the statue of Athena Parthenos by Pheidias once stood (438 B.C.); the sculpture on the stonework and gables (the remnants can be seen on the west gable), the metopes (page 79), as well as the frieze (page 77), stem from the same master (for his portrait see page 109).

28. Festive processions, the believers and the animals to be sacrificed, entered through the gateway (Propylaea) of the Acropolis, which Mnesicles of Athens built as a great festive entrance, consisting of porch and side wings.
Above: A view of the entrance hall, with Doric columns in the foreground and Ionic columns inside (page 81, details page 79–81).
Below: The great Propylaea of the sanctuary of mysteries in Eleusis were built as a faithful copy of the entrance hall to the Acropolis, when Marcus Aurelius was ordained. View from the south, in the background the pavement of the outer courtyard. More about Eleusis on pages 33–34.

29. The temple of Hera is the oldest in Olympia and according to tradition was already founded by 1096 B.C. The parts that remain are not earlier than 700 to 600 B.C. Columns standing on two tiered foundations surround the Cella. Only the base is built of stone, the rest is a framework of clay bricks dried by the sun. Inside stood the images of Hera and Zeus (page 3), and in a side niche one of Hermes by Praxiteles (page 10). The temple of Zeus was consecrated and begun during the first Olympic games after the Persian Wars, and was completed in 456 B.C. The master builder was Libus of Elis. The temple was destroyed by an earthquake during the Christian era and all that remains today are the foundations. The picture shows the base of the outer columns (peristasis), the remains of the inner columns with a marble border, and in front of it a pavement of black and white plates which leads to the image of Zeus by Pheidias (page 199).

30. The Erechtheum on the Acropolis lay to the north of the Parthenon, close to the former citadel wall. Against the austerity of the Doric Parthenon the Erechtheum presented many examples of the Ionic style: in the center the Cella with six columns in the front facing east and a wall with windows facing west, on the right a small chapel with Caryatides (page 84), and left, on a lower level, the north portico (page 31 above).
Below: The island of Delos was the birthplace of Apollo and Artemis and was consecrated to them. But outside their actual sanctuaries there were, already in early times, holy places dedicated to other deities. Halfway to the top of Mount Cynthus (holy to Zeus), there is a small sanctuary dedicated to Hera: a simple temple overlies an older building.

31. Below: The north portico of the Erechtheum served as an entrance hall to the side door at the back, which led into the Cella and also as a monumental shelter for Poseidon's trident mark, which, according to Mythus, grew out of these rocks during the quarrel between the god and Athena over the ownership of Attica. It could be seen at all times through an opening in the floor of the north portico.
Below: The temple of Nike on the Acropolis in a small Amphiprostyle with Ionic columns on both fronts. A frieze of figures over the entablature surrounds the building. An image of the Goddess of Victory once stood in the Cella. The temple is one of the most elegant ever built in the Ionic style.

32. The sanctuary of Apollo in Delphi is situated on a steep incline of the Phaedriades, the foothills of Parnassus (page 155). The winding holy way paved with large stones climbs the mountain. Soon after the battle of Marathon (490 B. C.), the Athenians erected a treasure house for precious offer-

ings; they placed it in a dominant position, on a curve of the holy way. The house was rebuilt by French experts after the excavations of 1903–1906. It is an antae temple in Doric style with sculptured metopes on which were depicted the deeds of Theseus opposite those of Heracles.

33. In many places wells and holy springs lay in front of the actual sanctuaries. There the faithful cleansed themselves before entering the precinct. In Eleusis the old well has been preserved; it stems from the time of Peisistratus and was protected by a roof. In Delphi the centuries have brought some changes to the mountain spring called Castalia: below the spring stands a basin hewn out of the rock, above it is a smooth wall with niches for offerings. Myths about this fountain have been created up to the present day. The old spring still gushes forth in unabated strength and provides water for the olive plantations in the neighborhood.

34. Outside the sanctuary of Apollo on the road from Delphi to Boeotia lay a town settlement, on the outskirts of which the travelling writer Pausanius, who described Greece for interested Romans in 200 B.C., found a sanctuary of Athena. To this belongs the circular building, the pillars of which have just been rebuilt. It is called a Tholos, is built in Doric style, and contains pedestals for statues. It is the work of Theodorus of Phokaea, a master builder of Attic tradition. In 400 B.C. Pericles commissioned Iktinos, the original builder of the Parthenon, to enlarge and improve the Telesterion at Eleusis (page 28). The inner sanctum was supported by numerous columns, and the participants of the mystic rites sat on the stone steps around them. The building also boasted a raised gallery, which was reached by outside steps hewn from the rock (above right).

35. The sanctuary of Zeus at Olympia was called Altis by the ancient Greeks, which means sacred grove. The trees inside the sanctuary have always been a landmark of the shrine at Olympia. The trees growing there today convey the impression of the once holy grove. In this grove Philip II of Macedonia founded a hieron after the battle of Chaeronea (page 291), which his son, Alexander the Great, completed. It is a circular building similar to the one in Delphi (page 34). In the inner sanctum stood the images of Alexander, his father and grandfathers and their wives. In this building the Macedonian monarchy was venerated. Because the Olympic games were part of the feast held in honour of Zeus, the sports ground or stadium was included in the holy precinct. The picture shows the direct entrance to the stadium; the vaulting was later added by the Romans.

36. In the lonely mountain ranges along the west coast of Attica lie the almost forgotten holy underground grottoes of ancient times. Narrow steps in the cliff lead nearly twenty feet below the ground. In the half darkness can be seen an altar, and the figures of a sitting goddess and a man with hammer and gauge. This is the stonemason Archidemus, who tells of himself in the inscription. Everything is hewn out of the rock including the numerous niches for sacrifices and oblations.

37. The mighty lions forming an avenue stand like guards upon their pedestals and look towards the holy sea, where Leto after much wandering gave birth to Apollo under a palm tree. The lions are examples of earliest Greek sculpture. Semicircular seats with backrests and capitals of columns in front are often to be found as offerings in ancient sanctuaries.

38. The tripod, which the Greeks consecrated after their victory over the Persians at Plataea (479 B.C.), once stood on a round pedestal at the top of a flight of stairs right at the end of the holy way in Delphi. The tripod was supported by snakes of which some remains can still be found in Istanbul.

39–41. The climax of Roman belief was the veneration of the trio in the Capitol: Jupiter, Juno, and Minerva. The Romans erected a Capitol, similar to the one in Rome, within colonized cities as a sign of unquestionable ownership, which shows to what extent religion and state were intertwined, making in fact a state religion, so that the gods represented the state itself. The Capitol of Ostia, built against the side of the Forum, is surrounded by the walls of the Forum, as a sanctuary is surrounded by its wall (page 39). The sacred and the profane are here completely united. Following the old Italo-

Etruscan custom, Roman temples are usually built on a podium which raises them high over their surroundings (pages 39–41, 90, 91). The sacrificial altar stands exactly in front of the outside steps leading to the temple, and forms a unity with the building because of their common axis. Because of the lack of space there are no halls in the sacred precinct of Vespasian in Pompeii (page 39). They have been reduced to a wall containing many niches, whereas on the plain of Baalbeck the generosity of a planned layout could be fully exploited (page 40). Sacred Roman architecture in Syria can serve as an example of Roman behavior; they transplanted their styles of building to the conquered lands and then merged them with native customs (page 41). Most temples in Syria contained an "adytum" (a place for an image heightened by a pedestal), with an outside staircase and a stone baldachin (canopy); it was the sacred goal of the whole sanctuary. The pedestal is hollow and contains a simple room – a crypt – which is reached through a door in the front of the adytum. Crypts, heightened pedestals, and canopies were the ancient forerunners of the Christian crypt and choir.

42. The subterranean shrine of a religious sect – followers of Pythagoras and Orpheus – which was discovered in front of the Porta Maggiore, consists of a hall with three naves of almost equal height. Enormous pillars support the vaulted ceiling. Special points of interest are the apse at the end of the central nave, and the rich stuccoes on the ceiling (page 221) which depict the religious beliefs of the sect, which differ in some instances from the "official" religion.

43. This charming relief shows a family visiting a sanctuary. The throned God (Asclepius?) and a female companion are on the right. The trunk of the great plane tree is covered with ornamental sashes, and on top of a high column stands an ancient group of figures. The devout family has approached the altar and even the youngest carries an offering.

Below: This relief is from one side of a square base on which stood an offering donated by three Phylarcae of Athens (district supervisors), after their district's victory in a horse race. The inscription names the artist Bryaxis, who came from Caryae but worked in Athens.

44. The sanctuaries gave asylum to fugitives: Orestes, pursued by the Erinnyes (one of them with wings and snakes can be seen on the left) because of his mother's murder, has fled to Delphi. He sits on a stone threshold embracing a holy tripod. Apollo and Athena are present as an indication of the forgiveness to come. It is the work of the Cassandra painter who came from Campania. Second half of the fourth century B.C.

Below: The picture shows the corner of an altar with pedestal and volutes. A man is kneeling in front of it and raking the ashes of the fire for the burnt offering. The standing figure in richly decorated gown and garlanded is performing the functions of a priest. He is about to make an offering of wine from a jug (page 14, 233). The ceremony is accompanied by a gesture which is similar to the one used in prayer, but executed with the left hand. Other forms of altars are on pages 51, 168, 244, 304.

45. The actual praying gesture is made with the right hand. The supplicant stretches out his arm to shoulder height and turns his palm towards the deity. That is how it is presented by the archaic artist. Some decades later however, the hand is drawn back, the head bent, and the general posture has changed from a formal to a relaxed attitude.

46. The usual description of work, which according to the figure of speech of Roman republican art represents an Etruscan as "Arringatore," explains the lifted hand as the gesture used for an address, similar to the adlocutio, the address of a general to his troops (page 116, 202). The hardly differentiated position of the fingers, however, points to the figure as being a supplicant.

47. A worthy Roman matron is shown wearing a simple peplos with a border which is drawn from the back over the head as a veil; in her hair is a diadem. In her lowered right hand the woman carried a bowl, in her left is a reproduction of a religious figure. The inscription in Boeotic script names Polyxena as inhabitant of the tomb. The stele is in the form of an aedicula (No. 298).

48. The ring with the round medallion and star indicates that the old man is a priest of the Egyptian goddess Isis, who was widely venerated in late Roman times. As a work of art this outstanding figure belongs to the period of Roman portraiture (A.D. 300), which created characters of exceptional expression (page 120).

49. The Vestals (priestesses serving Vesta) lived cloistered lives in the Atrium Vestae by the Forum in Rome. The only man allowed to enter their sanctum was the Pontifex Maximus, the high priest (No. 52), who was later generally identical with the emperor (see page 120, the portrait found in the Atrium Vestae of Gallienus). The Vestals remained virgins and were attired like brides at a wedding. Above the hair on the forehead lies a diadem and over it a sash wound round and round the head (infula), with the ends lying on the breast. On top of all this they wear a head scarf which is fastened by a brooch (fibula) in the front. The Museo Nazionale in Rome has several portraits of chief Vestal virgins.

50. A young veiled woman sitting on a cushion, perhaps at a wedding, takes incense from a shallow box (Pyxis, see page 297) in order to scatter it over the small bowl of an incense burner (thymiaterion); after the offering has been made, the hanging lid of the box would be closed again. The relief is from the side of a Greek altar, on the front of which the birth of Aphrodite is depicted (page 16).

51. A consular diptych is a small folding ivory tablet which the consuls, when they took up office in late Roman times, used to give away as presents. The outer side is ornamented with carvings (page 70-71) of the priestesses of Ceres (Demeter) on the left, and of Bacchus (Dionysus) on the right, making a ceremonial offering in the front of the altar in a sanctuary, which is indicated by trees (page 43). The torches belong to the service of Demeter (page 12). On the round altar of Ceres burns a fire. For the shape of the voluted altar see the Grabara (page 304).

52-53. The great Altar of Peace from the Field of Mars in Rome consisted of a wall surrounding an open courtyard and the actual sacrificial altar. Today the Ara Pacis Augustae is next to the Augustae Mausoleum (page 393) on the Tiber, and has been completely restored around the original pieces. The wall is ornamented inside and out and surrounded by a rich frieze. The reliefs on the outside depict the festive procession of the year 13 B.C. in which the emperor himself appears, preceded by lictors and followed by the four flamines (page 52) with their characteristic headgear (apex, see page 55), and the victimarius with the hatchets (Sacena) on their shoulders. The veiled supplicant on the right may be recognized as the Pontifex Maximus. The strict festive order of the official procession is somewhat softened by the presence of the emperor's family including the children (page 53). The Ara Pacis represents the most magnificent example of Augustan state art. The head on page 117 stems from the same work.

54-55. A pig (sus), a lamb (ovis), and a bull (taurus), used to be sacrificed to Mars at the Suovetaurilia, the festive state offering on the Field of Mars (Campus Martius). On the relief from the base of Domitius Ahenobarbus in Paris (page 54 above), Mars himself attends the sacrifice. He stands by the altar; music accompanies the ceremony. Roman sacrificial rites were held according to strict rules. On the relief on page 55, the emperor, with his toga over his head (see also page 236), scatters incense, which an attendant is holding out for him in a small casket (page 54), over a small tripod (Camillus, page 56). In front of the emperor is the flamendiales with the apex (No. 52), in front of the bull the flute player (tibicen), and next to him the Popa, who will hold and sacrifice the bull.

56. Camilli are boys who minister at a sacrifice. The Romans liked them to be well built and to come from good families. They wear a tunic with wide sleeves; the wine jug and sacrificial dish indicate their office (see also page 224).

THE THEATER

Pages 57–75

Since Thespis, the priest of Dionysus from Icaria in Attica, produced the first dramatic play with chorus, chorus leader and one actor, – in the year 534 B.C. during the great feast of Dionysus in Athens, all such plays, tragedies as well as comedies, were connected with the worship of Dionysus; just as the play was part of the ritual celebrations, so was the stage, the theatron, part of the whole sanctuary.

The theater in Athens originally stood where the remains still stand today: on the southern slope of the Acropolis. But the stone foundations date back only as far as the 4th century B.C. by which time the Attic tragedies were in decline. Before that time the plays were performed in the same grounds the Greeks used for dancing and on raised wooden stages. The audience sat on natural slopes, and it was the words, the poetry, and the movement of the chorus, not the spectacle which carried them along. In the 4th century theaters were erected in other places apart from Athens. While the building in Athens underwent many alterations up to Roman times, the theater in Epidaurus lies unaltered before us.

The focal point of Greek theater is the circular orchestra where the chorus performed (page 57). It is encircled by a stone ring and a narrow paved path. In the middle stands an altar called the thymele. The second part, the skene, a stone foundation for the superstructure of a stage, is laid out at a tangent to the circle of the orchestra. Facing it, cut into a natural slope, is the great round auditorium, with stone steps as seats, separated into tiers by a flight of stairs. The tiers on the upper third are divided by a corridor (diazoma). A Greek theater has no enclosing wall, the seats simply come to an end, for the Greek theater always maintained its relationship to the landscape: the arena is a monumental mounting of a natural hollow. From the tiers the eye can roam the countryside; in Athens the road lies on the left and the sea on the right. The Greek theater was always an open air theater. A covered theater also existed, the Odeum, but it was used for musical performances and competitions, not for drama. As early as the 4th century B.C. the domination of the chorus gave way to the plot, probably because the meaning of the chorus had been completely lost. After the degeneration of the song, the movement of the chorus in the orchestra became more limited and the shape of the orchestra was therefore changed: in Athens it is no longer a full circle, in Roman theaters only a half circle.

The parts of the classical Greek theater stand next to each other but are almost unconnected, bound together only by the power of the play and the sacred festival.

The Roman theater, on the other hand, is an enclosed entity: the many seats are erected on a superstructure unconnected with a natural hollow and the top gallery encloses the whole arena (page 59 below). The parodos, the entrance for the chorus (page 57 above), is vaulted (page 60) and connects the auditorium with the stage, making it into a spacious unity. Very characteristic are the turrets over these entrances (e.g. in Orange, page 59 above) which lend cover and depth to the stage. The stage building now has two stone facades: one on the inside, with three or five recesses serving as a backcloth, the other on the outside presenting the closed front of the theater to the town. By contrasting Greek and Roman theaters it is possible to recognize the whole fundamental difference in the trends of Greek and Roman architecture. There is another type of building, also stemming from religious roots which were later severed: the Roman amphitheater. The amphitheater forms an oval around a stage serving many purposes. The marvelous, outward facing fronts have served as examples for similar buildings throughout the ages and up to the present time; arched passages lie one above the other, in purpose no less Roman than in monumental expression; wisely thought out, these arcades solve the problem of the coming and going of large crowds. Each entrance below is numbered and leads to only one group of seats without touching any others.

57.   The theater of Epidaurus is by far the best preserved in Greece. It is continually being repaired and recently the parodostor (above right), through which the chorus made their entrances and exits, has been rebuilt to correspond with the old position on the opposite side. In the summer months productions of ancient drama can be seen here. The structure is distinguished by marvelous acoustics which, surprisingly enough, are also a characteristic of nearly all Greek theaters even when, as in Pergamum, the majority of the stone seats are no longer there.

58.   The theater on the southern slope of the Acropolis, north of the sanctuary of Dionysus (it can be seen on the top of the picture) underwent many changes right up to the time of Hadrian, especially the orchestra which, once round, is now almost semicircular. On the front of the stage are reliefs connected with the cult of Dionysus. Around the orchestra ran a canal covered with ornamental tiles (picture below left), to lead away the down-pouring water. A barrier of vertically placed flagstones divided the orchestra from the passage below; here the seating began with three rows of marble chairs on which the priests of the various gods and other high ranking persons (the so-called Proedria) used to sit. The seat for the priest of Dionysus in the front of the picture is distinguished by volutes on the front and armrests. The angular stands further up served as pedestals for the statues of Roman emperors.

59.   In Southern France, the Roman "Provincia," several theaters have remained well preserved; recently the tiered stone seats have been repaired and in many cases renewed, and the buildings have been partly reconstructed because the theaters are again being used for the performance of plays. All that remains of the "Scenae Frons" today is a bare brick or stone wall, which was once disguised by rich marble architecture. This was built up in three stories to represent a palace facade with three or five doors. The structure and regularity of the stage can still be recognized in the picture above.

60.   It is characteristic of the theater in Pompeii that a natural hollow was not used. The tiered stone steps of the auditorium were supported by foundations and therefore a buttressed outer wall, similar to that of the amphitheater, was included.

61–63.   The great amphitheaters of the Romans met a great need, especially during the time of the emperors, when the rulers presented spectacles for the people, such as the baiting of animals and the combats of the gladiators. These could not be put on the raised stage of the theater, but played on the wide flat surface of the arena. That is why the inner oval is surrounded by the stone seats in wide elliptical circles. Structures of this kind can be found throughout the whole Roman Empire, less in Ancient Greece than in other countries where the Romans found no other cultures.

The amphitheaters had to be planned to hold great numbers of people. The Colosseum in Rome (page 62) was calculated to hold 50,000. The outside face generally consists of three stories; the fourth story of the Colosseum (page 62) was added at a later time. It is a blank wall with brackets for masts, on which a huge canopy could be hoisted. The Colosseum was consecrated in the year 80 A.D., as the Amphitheatrum Flavium, by Vespasian; the inaugurating games lasted one hundred days, during which 5,000 wild animals were hunted in the arena.

64.   The performance of the classical tragedies outside Athens and especially in Magna Graecia after the 5th century B.C., greatly affected the decoration of vases, as is shown by the fragment in Dresden: the painting probably represents a scene from "Tereus," a lost drama by Sophocles. Tereus, clad in the theatrical costume of a king storms out of the palace door, center, in pursuit of his wife Procne and her sister Philomela who have served him his own son to eat. Paintings on vessels showing the effect of the comedies and satires were already common in ancient times. A chorus from a comedy is represented below: men disguised as horses, with horses' heads and tails, bend forward with the riders on their shoulders; they leap onto the stage, accompanied by flute music.

65.   Phlyacography is a form of burlesque originating from southern Italy. The players were dressed in burlesque costume, consisting of shoes, long hose, a padded top garment with hanging phallus, and a grotesque mask. There are numerous vases from Lower Italy depicting scenes from these plays (phlyacography vases). The vessel pictured above is a mixing bowl by Assteas, who painted in Poseidonia (Paestum) towards the end of the 4th century B.C. The painting represents a thieves' comedy: Charinos, a wealthy old man, is guarding his coffer of gold, two ruffians pull him away and steal his money. A moaning, frightened servant is helplessly standing by. In the field above, two female masks and a wreath.

Below: Originally, all actors, including the poets themselves, were amateurs, but soon it became a profession in which the star system was not unknown. They were well paid and enjoyed great popularity although they were not held in social esteem, especially by the Romans. The old mime actor is beautifully shown on the Dresden relief.

66.   Dioscurides of Samos is the artist who copied the work of an unknown (to us) Greek master of the 3rd century B.C. He made the copies in mosaic for the floors of Cicero's villa outside the Gate of Hercules in Pompeii. With the decline of the chorus songs, the music and dancing between the acts, especially in the new Attic comedies, gained in importance. It is probable that such an interlude is here being represented, because the two musicians are wearing the national costume of "Nea." The original picture was almost certainly on a consecrated tablet in a sanctuary, offered by a troup of musicians of whom one is here represented: a tambourine player (page 257), surrendering to the tone and rhythm of the music, wearing a youthful mask above which his own hair can be seen.

67.   An actor of phlyacography (page 65), with a torch in his right hand, apparently a parody of the tragic entrance; parodies and travesties were often part of these burlesques. He is wearing lovely, colored shoes.

68.   Masks were used in every Greek as well as Roman play. The use of masks, like the whole play, is religious in origin and stems from Dionysus who was himself worshipped wearing a mask. The masks were almost certainly not used as megaphones, as is sometimes thought, because the excellent acoustics of the Greek theater made it unnecessary to amplify the natural tone. The classical names for the masks, prosopon and persona, are synonymous with the word for "person." The expression and shape of the masks differed according to the kind of play in which they were being used.

69.   Myrina in Asia Minor was, after Boeotia, the center for the fabrication of terra cotta figures. Types from the comedies were a favorite subject in ancient times, and were displayed in the home from the 4th century B.C. Weighed down by an assortment of baggage, the returning warrior nevertheless marches happily along, struggling with his load. As a "Bramarbas" he would have much to tell about all kinds of adventures and was therefore an established comedy figure.

70.   For consular diptych see No. 51. The baiting of wild animals (the venatio) was presented as a spectacle for the amusement of the onlookers. On the left, lions in the arena being baited and killed by men wearing tunics and protective clothing and using simple hunting spears. On the right five stags

about to be defeated by one man, for the men in the open doors of the cages have no weapons to help the champion. Above the curve of the arena are the patron and judges of the games.

71–75. On the ivory tablet at right, the Byzantine emperor Anastasius (491–518 A.D.) is depicted sitting on his throne and with his raised right hand giving the signal for the games to begin. The picture below shows a fight between wild bears and men. The men are in a wicker cage which is being turned on a stake. The bears used for this purpose were captured in nets, like the stags (page 186). The hunter on page 186 is also returning with a chained bear to be used for baiting. The diptych at left shows a chariot race in the circus using teams of four horses abreast (quadrigae) at the moment of rounding the metae (cone shaped pillars placed at each end of the oval circus). The four competitors (factiones circenses) are shown entering one at a time onto the mosaic from the Villa of the Septimians (page 74). The factions or stables are distinguished by the color of their tunics; there was therefore a white, a red, a blue and a green faction. The cording around their bodies served as protection in the event of a fall (see also page 75). The equipment of a charioteer (auriga) also included a crash helmet (pages 71–75) and a long whip like those used today, held in the right hand (pages 71–74). The relief in Foligno (pages 72–73) is Roman folk art and therefore uninfluenced by considerations of representing the state. The relief shows in a fresh and observant style the four chariots neck and neck at the turning point, the furnishings of the circus and the spectators, platform with the patron's box. The relief, page 74, above, does not depict a caricature of a chariot race, but a spectacle which was really offered for the amusement of the people: a trained monkey confidently and cleverly steers a chariot with a team of two camels (biga) around the circus. Undoubtedly he too was given tumultuous applause.

BUILDINGS

Pages 76–103

Greek architecture consists mainly of temple architecture. Certainly there was also an extensive profane architecture which included fortifications (page 88), dwelling houses (page 212), palaces, gates, halls, markets, and sports grounds (pages 155–156), but their forms were developed from sacred architecture. The Greeks created three "orders" of architecture: the Doric, the Ionic, and the Corinthian. It is better to speak of "orders" than of "styles" in architecture because by style we understand an artistic expression limited to a certain time, while orders, in spite of changes wrought by style, retain their basic pattern. The word "order" here chosen follows the example of Vitruvius, a Roman author who wrote a work "About Architecture" in 25 B.C. in which he uses the Latin word ordo (Greek: ergasia).

A temple of the Doric order is markedly different from an Ionic one: although both generally have a three-tiered foundation, the Doric Column stands directly on the floor surface (stylobate, pages 76, 83, compare also pages 156, 212, 218), while the Ionic is separated from the floor surface by a profiled base (page 82). The Doric order therefore exploits the hard contrasts between the vertical and horizontal, the Ionic, on the other hand, softens and modifies the contrast. The same intention can be seen in the pillar head (capital): sharp edges on the abacus of the Doric (page 80), soft, elastic, whirling, volutes on the Ionic capital (page 81). The entablature over the Doric column consists of a simple heavy stone beam (epistyle or architrave) with the triglyph above it (pages 76, 78, 79, 80, 83), the Ionic entablature, on the other hand, has a beam with three horizontal recesses (pages 81, 84, compare page 31), as does the Corinthian architrave (page 84 below).

Sometimes a frieze of figures is also included (pages 30, 31, 83). The triglyph consists of two indentations which separate three moldings from each other. It is framed by a metope on each side. As the three moldings always lie above the center of a pillar, i. e. over the center of the transom of a pillar (pages 27, 32, 78, 80), they stress the vertical of the building. Conversely, friezes and horizontally faced Ionic beams form horizontal lines around the building (pages 30–31). Doric buildings produce a heavy, serious, grand, effect; Ionic ones, especially in the classical time of the fifth century B.C., were fine, delicate, and elegant. The Peloponnesus, where the Doric order originated, is also where it is chiefly to be found. The Ionic order of ancient times belonged to the Ionic Isles and the province of Asia Minor. Later both orders spread outside their fields of origin. The Corinthian order was "invented" in the second half of the 5th century B.C. It is of Ionic inclination regarding the base, the pillar shaft, and partly the entablature. The important distinguishing point is the capital. It appeared originally as an isolated capital, was integrated into rows of columns to be seen inside temples in the 4th century B.C., and only in the 3rd century B.C. did the order become used for the outside (page 84). The Corinthian capital (page 85) has in the center a chalice (calathos), round which lie parts of a flower, acanthus leaves, making a certain rhythmic pattern – a novelty in Greek art. Out of the leaves grow small volutes (helices) which carry a flower on the inside, while the outside verges upon the ceiling (abacus). The orders created by the Greeks retain their validity through the ages up to the time of the renaissance and even today, although modified, of course, and partly changed, the essence remains the same. The Doric order has clearly declined, the Ionic has remained in use, but the use of the Corinthian has greatly increased.

The main achievements of Roman architecture are not found in temple architecture but in the spheres of the great space formations (sanctuaries, forums), of the large baths (thermae), of the theater such as the amphitheaters (page 61), of triumphal arches (page 92), city gates (page 83), fountains, aqueducts and above all in the sphere of town planning, examples of which can be seen in Pompeii and Ostia and a few also in the African colonial towns. The domination of the Greek orders spread to the Roman temples, although they did not greatly alter the original style; i. e. the projecting podium with outside staircase (page 39), the deep portico (page 90) and the facing of the temple towards the front, in contrast to the Greek peripteral which is surrounded by columns. The orders employed, however, were Greek. The Roman temple, therefore, presents a strange mixture: around the ancient Roman, Italian, or Etruscan core falls the mantle of ancient Greece.

76. The Doric peripteral is a building with an elongated cella which is surrounded by halls of pillars on all four sides. The classical relationship between the narrow and long side is 6:13 (Parthenon 8:17). The Hephaesteum of Athens, the temple in which Hephaestus and Athena were jointly venerated, lies on the Colonos Agoraios, a medium-sized hill on the north side of the Agora of Athens. It is the best preserved temple in Greece because it was converted into a church of St. George and therefore escaped the general destruction. It is incorrectly known as the Theseum.

77. The steps of the substructure of the Parthenon are far too high to have been built for normal use, but the absolute greatness of the building demands such high steps. Lower in-between steps were therefore inserted on the narrow sides. The front edges of the steps do not form a completely precise horizontal; they rise towards the middle and fall away towards the ends. These are "curvatures," which lend the building art organic liveliness, and are pleasant to the eye. The frieze (above) is of the Attic-Ionic

order, but is here part of a pure Doric building. The blocks above the frieze, and the rectangular ones adjoining, formed the base for the coffers which covered the ceiling of the colonnade (peristasis).

78. Metopes are the smooth or sculptured panels between the triglyphs (page 79). The ones in the Parthenon showed reliefs on all four sides. Those from the south side depicting the battle of the Centaurs are now in the British Museum, together with other Parthenon sculptures ("Elgin Marbles"). Only the first south metope remained in its place. The head pictured on page 109 stems from this metope.

79. The metopes on the Hephaesteum (page 76) are smooth except for those around the portico which are sculptured; shown here is the north side depicting the battles of Theseus.
Below: Antae are shaft-like projections or endings of the wall. In the Doric order the anta capital is simply profiled (for the Ionic see page 82).

80–81. In general appearance the Propylaea of the Acropolis are of the Doric order, but although the east and west fronts, as well as the wings, are Doric, the high hall inside is Ionic. This mixture of the two orders is significant in its effect on the history of Greek architecture.

82. The rich antacapital from Miletus belongs to the Ionic order. The contour is simple but the surface is richly ornamented. The ornamentations increase in size towards the top: a small molding (astragal) at the bottom is followed by a small Ionic cyma, a band of hanging palmettes and a large cyma covered by a plain panel (abacus). The Ionic column base from the north colonnade of the Erechtheum (page 31) consists of two bulges and one indentation. The top bulge (torus) was enriched by a plastic intertwining band.

83. Storied buildings became generally known in Hellenic times. Shown here is the entrance to the Athena Sanctuary of the upper citadel of Pergamum: the heavy Doric order has been used below, the lighter Ionic order above, which was in accordance with the custom of the time. There is a marble balustrade between the Ionic columns with reliefs depicting looted weapons.

84. In front of the south side of the cella of the Erechtheum is a building called the Corae. Corae are maidens who, as caryatids, support the beams in the place of pillars or columns.
Below: The temple of Zeus Olympius, the Olympium in Athens (page 26), was first begun in 530 B.C., under the "tyrant Peisistratus" as a dipteros, a temple surrounded by a double peristyle. The Ionic building was left unfinished. In Hellenic times (2nd century B.C.) more was built on the old ground plan but in the Corinthian order, which was modern at that time. The building was only finished under the Emperor Hadrian. The remaining group of columns stems from the southeast corner of the building.

85. The example stems from the circular building (Tholos) called "Thymela" in the Asclepieum at Epidaurus. On the outside it was a magnificent example of the Doric order; on the inside, of the Corinthian. The special features of the capital shown make it probable that it was used as a pattern for the stonemasons, that it never became part of the building and that it was buried as it was, after the completion of the building, which would perhaps explain its marvelous preservation. Below: "The Tower of the Winds" stands in front of the Roman agora (market place) in Athens. Andronicus of Macedonia had it built at his own expense as a clock tower: inside the time of day was read from the water level in pipes, the outside had sundials on each side. The reliefs on the upper part of each side of the octagon represent the Gods of the Winds (hence the name now used), according to the directions from which they blow. Their names are inscribed. Beams divide the inside into stories; an upper gallery with Doric half columns supports the slanting roof, which consists of board-like marble wedges, laid side by side.

86. Gutter spouts, mainly in the shape of animal heads, were used to drain the water which collected in the gutters under the eaves of the temple. The water flowed to the ground through their hollowed mouths.

87.   Temple pediments counted as an invention of the Corinthians. Their surface was usually covered with groups of figures (see Aegina, pages 136–137). Over the center and the corners of the pediment stood "acroteria," ornamental figures (page 9). The one shown here is the center acroterium of an Etruscan temple, depicting a winged creature carrying off a child.

Below: The terra cotta or marble bricks of the temple were so laid that the joins ran from the crest of the ridge to the eaves. These joins were covered with tiles. Each row of covering tiles began with the ridge tile on top and ended on the eaves, over the cyma with a front tile (antefix). One of these is reproduced at the bottom of page 87: on a hollow palmette is the grimace of the Gorgon. An image of the Gorgon was said to have the power of warding off evil. This example is a work from Veii and originates from the time when Vulca of Veii worked on the temple from which the antefix stems.

88.   The Romans invented the "standard stone" of their age, i. e., square building stones of equal size. The Greeks, on the other hand, never used such simplified technical methods so that the liveliness of a Greek stone wall was preserved throughout the ages. This is illustrated by the lovely fable which tells of Amphion and Zetos, two brothers, and sons of the king, who built walls around their town. One of them carried the heavy blocks of stones and laid one upon the other; but the other brother played the cithara so that the stones would blend harmoniously.

89.   The island of Delos is today as short of water as it was in ancient times. Therefore it has always been necessary to collect rain water in large walled-in containers. Every house in the town of Delos (pages 212–217) had such a cistern. The largest was by the theater (above). To judge from the ruins of the ancient library buildings, the library itself and the reading room were contained in a single room. The "books" – scrolls – lay in shelves on the wall. In Athens, as everywhere else, only the niches in the walls have been preserved.

90–91.   Only the basic structure of the speaker's rostrum (rosta) from the Forum Romanum has been preserved. It was richly covered in marble according to the custom of the time which favored the covering of bricks and walls with marble panels of many different kinds (incrustation).

92.   Triumphal arches were erected to commemorate past triumphs. The general, at the head of his army, rode through the wooden gates of the arch to expiate the blood shed in the war. Such arches are not only to be found in Rome and in other parts of Italy, but also in the provinces of the Roman Empire. The simple type has one single gateway; the more ornamental type has a high, wide, central gateway, with lower ones on the sides. The fronts are richly recessed and sculptured. Above is an "attic" with dedication, and on top of it the quadriga (chariot with four horses abreast) with the triumphant general. The relief ornamentation of the triumphal arch of Constantine in Rome originates mainly from monuments erected by earlier emperors, which were later destroyed. This arch was erected in 312 A.D. in memory of the triumph of the Emperor after his victory over Maxentius at the Milvic bridge which became the victory of Christendom. On the arch itself there are, of course, no kind of Christian symbols. The Emperor was only baptized on his death bed in the year 337 A.D.

93.   The name "Porta Nigra" came into being only in the 12th century and applies to the color of the weathered stone. It is the northern gateway of the city dating back to the time of Constantine and was the most important Roman fortification north of the alps. It also is significant because of its decorative and representative character, which is more highly developed than was usual in such fortifications. The picture shows the outside with the round towers projecting in front. On the left (i. e., on the east side) are the last preserved remains of the reconstructions of the middle ages, the chorapsis (12th century) of the Church of Simeon.

Below: The market gate of Miletus, which formed the monumental entrance to the southern market of the city, is also ostentatious for its purpose. The doors and stories of the facade are reminiscent of the stage fronts of Roman theaters (page 59).

94. The Greeks and Romans dedicated fountain houses to the nymphs. The vaulting, which became regular in later structures, is reminiscent of the vaults in natural caves where the nymphs were venerated. The recessing of the walls with well-placed niches is a typically Roman form of decoration.

Below: Roman aqueducts were laid overground as though symbolizing the peaceful might of the empire. The Pont du Gard is purely utilitarian but made beautiful by the rhythmic structure of its arches. This marvelous construction was required to bridge the river valley.

95. The Pirene of Corinth is age-old.

The river god Asopus presented it to King Sisyphus, the founder of Corinth. The winged horse Pegasus was drinking here when he was captured by Bellerophon. The fountain house dates back to the early Greek times. The well was in constant use and therefore frequently rebuilt. What we see today is late Roman; in front of the arched entrances and the old water chambers is a colonnade, at the foot of which lies a fountain.

96. Part of a relief from the tomb of the Haterii (Via Labicana in front of the Porta Maggiore in Rome, for examples of the same sepulcher see page 197). It represents a part of the holy way (via sacra) between the Forum and the Colosseum. The latter is shown in its original form, i.e., without the fourth story (page 67). The general effect is enhanced by the figures in the arched entrances with images of the gods with eagles above them.

97. Over-ornamentation of buildings leading to baroque obscurity was a characteristic of architecture during the time of the Roman emperors, especially the merging of Ionic volutes with the Corinthian chalice into a new composite order.

98-103. Town streets, which we have mainly come to know through the systematic excavations in Pompeii and Ostia (the port of Rome), generally run straight and on level ground, crossed at right angles by side streets, thus dividing the area of the town into certain quarters (insulae). The roads are paved with large irregular blocks. In Pompeii there are stepping stones to facilitate crossing without getting wet feet. The streets were built exclusively of stones and bordered by uninterrupted rows of houses built to make use of every inch of ground; there was no room left for a tree, let alone for front gardens. Most of the houses were built in stories, the fronts were enlivened by narrow entrances, windows, and also by rows of shops having only one door leading from the street (page 98 below). Balconies, which were once also to be found in Pompeii, are especially well preserved in Ostia (page 99 below). Large state-owned or private warehouses (horrea) are characteristic of the port of Ostia where there was a continuous turnover of merchandise (page 196). They were the imposing warehouses of large trading concerns dealing in all kinds of wares, not only corn and oil (page 100). Page 100 above shows the main entrance to a trading firm managed by two freedmen, Epagathus and Epaphroditus (Horrea Epagathiana). They left their names inscribed on the architrave of the vaulted entrance leading into an open, several storied, inner court from which the warehouse and living quarters were reached (compare with the courts on page 213). The numerous and varied inns were a feature of town life. The fishmonger's shop (page 102) consisted of a table, a tank for the fish, and marble covered counters mostly placed next to the entrance (page 101). Fireplaces and wine bars can be seen further inside the gaily painted crossvaulted eating house in the Via Diana (page 101 below).

The wealth of the merchants of Ostia is reflected in the club houses (page 102 below): The "scola del Traiano" belonged to a rich trading company; beyond the marble floor of the dining room (triclinium) can be seen a courtyard with a long, narrow, water basin. The elegant layout could be used for holidays and relaxation, and to enjoy companionship and conversation. Every Roman town had its thermae, public baths, of varying sizes; they served not only the cause of cleanliness and bodily care, but were also social meeting places for conversation and sport (page 103). The small and large latrines make it plain that even the sanitary arrangements catered for social life. The lavatories (page 103 below) around the edge of a marble paved courtyard consist of numerous marble seats without any separating walls; a gutter with running water provided the necessary sanitation. Towns like Ostia,

Pompeii, Herculaneum, Timgad in North Africa, but also Priene in Asia Minor and Olynthus in Northern Greece provide an almost inexhaustible source of information for our knowledge of town life and behavior in ancient times. Further pictures of these places are on pages 39, 60, 106, 196, 198, 203, 212–219, and 304.

POETS AND PHILOSOPHERS

Pages 104–112

When the Greeks wanted to paint or model their old poets, Homer, Hesiod, Alcaeus, and Sappho, or the early lyricists and philosophers before Socrates, they found that there was no record of their individual appearances. For although they had lived at a time when personality already had a certain meaning, the representation of individual physiognomical peculiarities was not part of the intention of the artistic trend of their age. Not until early classical times (480 B.C.) is there an inclination to represent – beyond the general timeless features – such distinguishing peculiarities as make it possible for the observer to recognize who it is. The head of Homer belongs to the first attempts in this field; the result was a classical formulation valid throughout the ages (page 104). In the beautiful picture on page 105, Alcaeus appears as a singer in the traditional costume, and the woman standing by him is an ordinary musician without any individual distinguishing marks, so that the identification of the couple as the poets Sappho and Alcaeus is solely dependent on the inscription. The case of Homer on the other hand and also of Aesop (about 550 B.C.) is different (page 106): the latter was malformed. He associated with animals as though they were men. The enormous head with receding hair – the face was almost a caricature – as well as the conversation with the fox, sufficed for him to be recognized. Homer was known to be old and wise, and, above all, he was known to be blind. Therefore the Greeks always from the early 5th century B.C. until the last decade of the first century A.D. represented him with the bodily infirmity of blindness. In early works it was made to seem as if his blindness had given him an inner sight (page 104), latterly it was shown in all pathological details. The earliest likeness of Homer of which we know – the Roman copies give us an excellent impression – was a sacred offering by Micythus of Rhegium, which stood in front of the temple of Zeus in Olympia and was the work of the otherwise unknown Dionysius of Argus. The tranquillity of the austere contours (page 104), comparable to the head of Zeus in Athens (page 2), encompasses the strength of the inner expression born out of the knowledge of the time (about 460 B.C.) about the essence of the poetical.

During the lifetime of Socrates, when Sophocles and Euripides were writing their tragedies, a new trend appeared in Greek art which took note, in a new way, of the visible realities of human life; it heralded the beginning of the art of portraiture. Thus the portraits of Sophocles and Euripides, of Plato, Socrates and others, can be traced back, although created after their deaths, to originals which were based on nature. They also still remained, of course, – true to the essence of the Greeks – a representation of character. By comparing the head of Sophocles (490–406 B.C., page 107), with its dignity and inner tranquillity, with the careworn face of the misanthropic Euripides (about 480 to 406 B.C., page 108 below) – two things can be recognized: the artistic trend of the time and the poetic character of the two tragedians manifest in their works. The physical appearance of Socrates, the traditional Satyr-like face, the head and short neck (page 109), are masterfully indicated. The relief depicting a composite group, with the philosopher who was known for his keen mind rather than his elegant figure, Diotima, known from Plato's "Symposium," and Eros, probably originates from the statue of Socrates by Lysippus which stood in the Pompeiium in Athens. Ernst Langholz (Bonn) assumes (with good reason) that the head of the Centaur on the first south metope of the Parthenon (page 78) is a concealed selfportrait of Phidias (page 109); the individual traits of the face, of the "Artist's head" half-buried behind the shoulder, are unmistakable. The head is, in any case, a masterpiece of characterization.

The philosophers, who since Plato's academy had grouped themselves around newly founded schools of different trends and systems and propagated their teachings, soon, in spite of individual characteristics, developed into certain types. Philosophers generally were not among the best-groomed personalities of Greek society – and it is exactly this quality which the artists repeatedly observed and represented (page 108–110). The long beards are part of the profession, and a certain "embonpoint" seems to have been a matter of course (page 110). Sarcasm, irony and biting wit belong to the philosophical attitude and are clearly shown in the facial expressions, but, above all, the character of the thinker dominates. The Greek philosophers were not only abstract thinkers who explored the universe in all directions but they also contributed to the founding of European science.

The statue of Demosthenes (384–322 B.C.) is outstanding among the portraits of orators which also originated in the 4th century B.C. It was not made until 40 years after his death – he died from poison by his own hand – and was erected in the market place in Athens; the austere sexagon of shoulders and arms rises above the bent head of the patriot whose passion, statesmanlike judgment, and oratory have been passed over by the course of history; it is a deeply affecting countenance.

104. The blindness of the poet – already represented and handed down by the Egyptians – is here marked by closed lids. The head, many copies of which had been preserved, was formerly thought to be Epimenides. Erich Boehringer has given detailed reasons for the correct contention that it is Homer.

105. This peculiarly shaped vessel, with the small handles on the side and the pipe-like outlet at the bottom, is the only one known of its kind. Alcaeus sings with his head bent, in contrast to the singer on page 249. The painter has plainly indicated that he is singing: five small red circles, like notes, issue from his mouth.

107. The cylindrical container standing on the right side of the figure contains book scrolls to indicate the poet (page 112, 227, 257). It is an addition on the copy, and was not present on the original Greek bronze.

108. This head was found in the sea by the island of Anticythira in 1900. The light eyes which shine out of the dark bronze are insertions of a different material, as was the custom (page 113, 174, 284, 285; empty hollow eyes from which the insertions are today lost; page 2, 114, 165, 175).

109. Eros holds a small chest (pages 222, 227, 233) from which Diotima has taken a sash. Socrates supports himself with a gnarled stick (compare No. 152); he is wearing sandals made of simple straps.

111. This statue was erected by the State of Athens at the instigation of Demochares, a nephew of Demosthenes. The orator is represented with his hands folded, and not carrying a book scroll, as in many other portraits.

112. This mosaic was found in Sarsina in Umbria. Seven scholars are gathered around a globe in the center. The original, after which the work was copied, belonged to the province of Hellenistic art. It has been many times restored.

STATESMEN

Pages 113–121

The statesmen, in Greek times, were the strategists (Generals) as well as the men in charge of running the supreme state departments. These political leaders were not always honored by statues. All the same the series of statues of strategists (bearded men with helmets on their heads) began soon after the Persian wars. One of these is the statue of a helmeted warrior from Sparta (page 124), even if it is questionable whether it represents Leonidas, the famous defender of the Thermopylae (480 B.C.). The Hellenistic epoch was the great time for statues of statesmen (3rd to 1st century B.C.). A statue of this kind always had a special function: to represent the state in the person of the ruler, and to make his power evident. But these statues were also portraits, i.e., reproductions of historic persons with their unique peculiarities, especially of the face, even if they were represented in a heroic pose (page 114) or were raised above day-to-day life by nakedness. Many of these Hellenistic statues, though preserving the character of portraits, pattern themselves – also politically – on the example of Alexander the Great. The emotion of the expression follows from this prototype, and is, on the other hand, also a sign of the baroque attitude of the Hellenistic epoch (page 113 above). Historically, Hellenic sculpture formed the basis for the Roman portrait to which was, of course, added the still stronger driving force of the deeply rooted religious need of the Etruscans and the Romans: to preserve the uniqueness of a person in a "likeness" for the family. Beyond the family circle, but derived from it, are the portraits of the Roman emperors, which, beginning with Augustus, are an almost complete series; comment and explanation are here mainly facilitated by comparison of the statues with the coins of the time (page 202). Nearly all the sculptures originated through the emperor himself, either expressly ordered or permitted by him. This is amazing, as the character of the ruler is often depicted with unsparing candor even if it was far from pleasant by our standards. A true likeness was more important to them than idealization, or "modification," for reasons of prestige. They wanted to be recognized in their portraits as living people and not as an abstract idea. Many copies were made of a statue or bust originating from the court, which were given as presents and sent as far as the most remote provinces where, again, further copies were made. The presence of the portrait was held – like a cult image – in almost equal esteem as the presence of the emperor himself. The Roman emperor cult outside Rome consisted of offerings to the state as personified by the emperor, and of the veneration of the emperor as a god; in Rome this happened only after the "consecration" i. e., after the declaration of the senate that the late emperor had ascended to the gods. This cult served to establish the spiritual leadership of the state and to strengthen what the weapons of the army and the might of the administration secured in the military and political spheres.

113.   This head almost certainly represents a "Diadoch," one of the many successors of Alexander, for private portraits were still rare in Hellenistic times although they did exist; for in "Character types" by Theophrastus (372–287 B. C.) the author describes the flatterer as a man who always finds the portrait of the landlord well done. This head from Delos is excellently preserved and is most impressive because of its moving pathos.
Below: The portrait depicts a man functioning as a priest; he is definitely a Greek, an Athenian, although he is beardless like the Romans (from the first century B. C.). The mental and spiritual characterization of the personality, penetrating, in spite of all control, into the art of portraiture, almost approaches the coinage of the Augustan period (pages 116–117).

114.   It is not known who was represented by the life-sized bronze statue, called the "Thermae Ruler" (found in the same place in Rome as the sitting pugilist, page 165). Various suggestions have been made but none of them is completely convincing. Because of the heroic stance it was thought to be a Diadoch or possibly a Roman general. The sculpture is the work of a Greek master about 150 B.C.

115.   The only authentic portraits of Caesar can be seen on the coins minted during the lifetime of the dictator. They differ greatly from the sculptured portraits because these were mostly made a long time after his death. The head shown here is an outstanding example from the time of Caesar, but it is questionable whether it is Caesar.

116.   The emperor Augustus (63 B.C. to 14 A.D.) is represented addressing the army (adlocutio, see No. 46), wherefore his right arm is raised. He is no longer young, although the signs of age have not been truly reproduced; he was probably between 45 and 50 when Livia, his wife, erected the statue in her villa next to the Via Flaminia in front of the city gates. It is a masterpiece of controlled Augustan art which was molded on the classical Greek pattern, thereby becoming the classical epoch of Roman art, which, in turn, formed the pattern for other epochs. According to E. Buschor (Munich) the statue is a purely Greek original.

117.   Youthful masculine beauty was – true to classical tradition – highly valued at the court of Augustus. The picture (and other things also) prove this: the graceful head of the young man originates from the northern frieze of the outer wall of the Ara Pacis Augustae. It is the head of a youth belonging to the emperor's retinue who looked back over his shoulder during the procession in the year 13 B.C. He was definitely not a "Statesman" but belonged to the court and was therefore included in the official representation of the feast (regarding the peace altar of Augustus see No. 52).

118–121.   Portraits of Roman emperors. The head of Claudius (page 118 above) is part of a statue depicting the emperor as Jupiter. The oak wreath, although generously restored, is well secured. The head of Nero (page 118 below) counts as one of the most beautiful portraits of this emperor. Sickle-shaped locks lie low on his forehead, the hooded eyes reveal his distrustful character, and the lines around the mouth his cruelty. The marvelous marble head of Trajan from Ostia (page 119 above) shows the soldierly nature of the emperor, on the one hand, and, on the other, seen from the artistic point of view, the turning away from the soft Flavian appearance of his predecessors (compare with the head of Nero page 118), and the turning towards the renewed classical inclinations of Hadrian (page 119)below. This emperor reintroduced the Greek fashion of beards which was assumed by many later emperors. With the Antonian emperors a new expression of character enters into the Roman portrait: a more realistic look due to the sculptured sunken eye (page 120). The texture of the hair also becomes more real, as the sculptor no longer depicts single curls but gives the impression as a whole. The head of Gallienus, which is part of a statue which once stood in the house of the Vestals as a personification of the Pontifex Maximus, is, in spite of being larger than life, full of penetrating characterization. Porphyry, which is difficult to work, and is reminiscent in its color of the imperial purple, was the material almost exclusively reserved for statues of emperors. This stone, as well as the dress, the diadem, and the orb, distinguish the figures as rulers. By their embrace they are shown to be co-regents (compare the similar porphyry group in front of St. Mark's in Venice), and supposed to be Diocletian and his co-emperor; the style is a beautiful example of late Roman sculpture.

MILITARY LIFE

Pages 122–145

The armor of a fully equipped Greek infantryman (hoplite) consisted of cuirass, greaves, helmet, shield and lance. Other weapons used were the bow and arrow, and, above all, the short sword. If the cuirass was made of metal its decorations consisted of ornamental indications of the shape of the human body, (chest, ribs etc. pages 125, 138), but usually the soldier wore a breastplate of leather, painted on the outside; frequently a broad ornamental band stretches across the front beneath the chest (pages 126, 127, 123). The cuirass covers the body like a jerkin from shoulder to hip; it was put on like a corset (page 122 below), and fastened at the sides (page 127), and on top by shoulder flaps (pages 122, 123, 126, 127). These consist of the flap itself over the whole width of the shoulder and a narrow strap for fixing. The shoulder flaps of Aristion and Achilles were adorned with a star (pages 126, 127), that of Augustus (who is wearing a cuirass, in shape not unlike a Greek one) is adorned with a sphinx, the original emblem of the Emperor's seal (page 116). A double row of leather strips hang from the lower edge of the breastplate (page 127) to protect the body, and below them can be seen the richly pleated costume, for the cuirass was worn over a short shirt-like garment (chitoniskos). (Compare also the sleeves, pages 123, 126 and others).

The hoplite always wore greaves to protect the shinbones, sometimes also to protect the thighs (page 122 above, pages 122, 123 and 280). The interior picture of the bowl on page 124, shows how they were put on: they fitted over the shin and calf without any special fastening.

The bronze helmet protects the whole head, leaving only small slits for the eyes and mouth. The Ionic helmet covers the face particularly closely (page 125). The helmets from the Greek mainland are distinguishable as either Corinthian or Attic; the Corinthian is made in one piece with a protruding neck part, fixed and tapering cheekpieces, oval slits for the eyes and a narrow bridge covering the larger part of the nose. Both the Corinthian and the Attic helmet have a large crest, fixed on a long stick, or riveted to the crown of the helmet. The Attic helmet is more elegant (pages 124, 136), though its protection is perhaps not quite so effective. It is mostly worn by Athena (pages 7, 8, 134, compare also the Amazons page 138). Its cheekpieces were often movable flaps on hinges (e. g. pages 123, 262, 280). Ornamented cheekpieces on the helmet of Leonidas, page 124.

There are two types of armored shields: the circular shield, and the oval shield with indentations at the sides (pages 122, 123, 127). When not in use it was kept in a leather cover (page 128); on the march it was simply slung over the back (page 124). A glance at the reverse side of the shield reveals the method of carrying it (page 251). A metal ring for the upper arm is fastened to the

XXX

shield by long bands; (many such bands were found during the excavations at Olympia); a criss-cross of bands and straps served as a firm grip for the hand (page 280). The emblems on the curved exterior were numerous, especially in archaic times; satyrhead (page 122), gorgoneion (pages 122, 262), snake (page 8), cock, kantharos, lion (page 208), a pride of fighting lions (page 123), a large eye (page 278); these emblems often spread over the whole curved surface, thus manifesting their apotropaic character which was to ward off and frighten the enemy. The long lance was used to thrust at the enemy from a distance, before proceeding to use the sword in close combat (page 138). The hoplite, as a rule, had two such lances at his disposal (pages 122, 128, 131). The javelin is shorter and was used both on horseback and on foot (page 133). There is generally some representative significance in portrayals of the "doryphoros," the "man with the lance." The spear is part and parcel of the Athenians' dignity as well as of the ancients' conception of Achilles (page 126, 127), who received the big lance from his mother Thetis (the famous portrait of the doryphorus of Polyclitus, seen on the relief from Argos, page 132, is also assumed to represent Achilles). Finally it is a symbol of majesty (see page 114 and "Alexander with the lance"). The sword is usually short (see pages 8, 44), pointed, and two-edged, equally apt for cutting or thrusting. It was kept in a leather sheath (page 262) and carried on a short strap running across chest and shoulder (page 127). Hunters, too, sometimes carried the short sword (page 185), using it as a cutting weapon (page 184), as did Hercules in fighting the Amazons (page 138).

The clothes of the warrior consisted of a short chiton and a cloak (page 127, inter alia, compare the lighter clothing on the march, pages 131 above, 128). The usual long distance weapon was the bow and arrow. The arrows were kept in a quiver which was carried on the back (page 130), or in battle also on the thigh. The Amazons were renowned archers. They were often depicted wearing a close fitting garment with sleeves, long trousers, and the "Phrygian" cap (page 130). The archers of the Greek army wore similar "oriental" dress as a uniform (page 129). The bow was strung by first gripping it between the legs (page 129 below) with the string attached to the lower end and then bending it and fastening the string to the other end. The arrow was shot from a lunging position (page 130), or the warrior with his left foot forward, both knees bent, and a slight flexing of the upper part of his body held the bow out in his left hand and pulled the string with his right (page 130). The footwear of the archer usually consisted of half-length boots with four flaps hanging down (page 129, footwear also page 133).

The horse in the Greek army was used both for riding and drawing the chariot (quadriga) (pages 134, 135); it carried the rider on the march (page 131) and apparently also served to parade: the handsome Leagros for instance is certainly not riding into battle but is out for a ride in order to be seen. Although cavalry as a military formation was of secondary importance in the battles of earlier times, horsemanship as such must be presumed to have been on a high level. Later, under the Macedonian kings, and particularly Alexander the Great, cavalry gained in importance, often deciding the battle. Under the Romans it formed an indispensable part of the army (pages 141, 152). It appears from the pictures that spurs came into use only at a later date (page 176).

122. This Amphora is one of the most beautiful made and painted by the Greek potter Exekias; it is immaculately preserved. The elegant inscriptions which form part of the whole composition

name Exekias, and the depicted heroes of Troy, as well as the favorite name Onetorides. A particularly fine cloak is represented by most elaborate engraving.

Below: Old Priam instructing the young Hector going into battle. His mother Hecuba holds his weapons ready (the same subject "Hector's farewell" page 280).

123. Neoptolemus was the son of Achilles. Odysseus furnished him with arms and conducted him to Troy because Troy could not be captured without him.

Below: Achilles is here represented as a youth, in contrast to the portrayal by Exekias a generation later (page 122 above). The circular composition of the scene is a masterpiece. Patroclus turns away from the painful procedure, propping his foot against the "wall."

124. The tombstone is comparatively wide, in contrast to the narrow "stele" (page 126). The Ionic volutes at the upper end were once crowned by a palmette which encased the elaborately reproduced Attic helmet. A hoplite is represented, collapsing as he runs: his head is lowered, the fingers of the clenched fist are loosening, his whole body is sinking; it is a masterpiece of Attic, late archaic, art.

Below: It is not certain whether this is Leonidas, but it is not unlikely. Only the upper part of the body has been preserved, from which it appears that the warrior was represented lunging forward (compare pages 136, 138, 189). On the cheekpiece of the helmet there is a ram's head in relief. The nudity of the man purports to idealize him, exalting him above the worldly sphere (similarly pages 124, 128, 129, 132), for at no time, of course, did a warrior fight naked.

125. The hair hanging down in long curls at the back conforms with the style of the time. It is the festive hair style, not worn in battle. Later on, the representation of hair styles was more closely adapted to reality, i. e. the hair was reproduced as short (e.g. page 126 and following).

126. This is a most elaborate relief. The tip of the beard was broken off during chiseling. It was then added by the artist as a separate piece but has now been lost again.

127. The vases of antiquity show many pictures obviously painted by the same master; the names of the artists, however, are often not known. Experts on vases, above all J. D. Beazley, have allocated invented names to the anonymous painters: this picture became the starting point for the collection of many paintings by the same master under the name of Achilles painter. He was one of the most prominent of the classical era.

128. Work of the Euaion painter of whom particularly slim figures are characteristic.

Below: Representations of warriors bidding farewell are among the most popular motifs of archaic and classical vase painting (see pages 134, 268, 278, 280). The soft hat in the nape of the neck was worn on the march and while travelling, and is therefore typical of Hermes, the messenger of the Gods (page 11). The young warrior in the picture has a slight beard on his cheeks (compare pages 158, 159, 160, 164, 167, 185, 249).

129. The implement lying in front of the archer is a battle-axe often employed in battle by the Amazons. For other shapes of the cap compare pages 130, 133.

131. For the rider's whip with the short stock and long thong compare the shepherd with the fur cap on page 241.

132. This relief created and discovered at Argos, the home of Polyclitus, combines the reproduction of a Polycleitian lance bearer (doryphoros) and a horse.

Below: The long band of the frieze of the Parthenon, running round the cella represents a procession of Athenians on the occasion of the Panathenaic festival, in honor of Athena Parthenos. The series starts at the south corner of the western frieze with the preparations for the arrangement of the procession: a man in chiton and chlamys (short cloak) is engaged in calming his rearing horse in order to be able to mount it and join the horsemen. A large contingent of Attic horsemen filled a considerable stretch of the frieze.

133. The harness of the horse is simple, though here adorned with a breast piece. The single rein was held in the left hand, as it is today, leaving the right hand free for fighting, or for carrying the lance or some other weapon.

134. The chariot was used to approach the enemy: it was drawn by four horses, therefore the driver has more reins in his hand. On the right buttock of the outside horse (below) a circular brand mark gives an indication of highly developed horse breeding.

135. The chariot on this part of the frieze of the Parthenon, dating from the classical period, is depicted in the same manner as in archaic times, i. e. wheel with nave and four spokes, body and winged side guards. The driver on the chariot stands leaning backwards, holding the reins. The young armed warrior is just about to jump from the moving chariot.

136–137. The gable sculptures of the Athena-Aphaia temple of Aegina were discovered in 1811 and acquired by the Bavarian Crown Prince Ludwig for the Glyptothek in Munich. They were then restored by no less an artist than Thorwaldsen. They are the remains of an east and a west gable erected about 500 B. C. The east gable was replaced in 480 B.C. by a new one. Bronzes found in Dodona are distinguished by a particularly beautiful, dark green patina.

138. Hercules fighting three Amazons with his sword. The quiver for the arrows is seen behind his right thigh, the lion skin is worn over the chiton, the lion's head like a helmet. The picture originated about 560 B.C. in Athens, from the school of the Antimenes painter, which was one of the most eminent.

139. Roman helmets worn on parade and on ceremonial occasions were richly adorned. The example above shows a human face on the forehead plate with curls above the eyes and at the sides. The following pages show the customary Roman helmets.

140–141. The column of Marcus (as well as that of Trajan) is still standing on its original site, today named Piazza Colonna. The large column consists of many single drums on which the incessant battles of the Emperor with the Sarmatians and the Marcomanii (171 to 175 A. D.) are depicted in a spiral band. At the top of the column which, including the pedestal, is 40 meters high once stood the figures of Marcus Aurelius and his wife Faustina, now replaced by the figure of St. Paul. The Roman soldiers wear scale armor which is a kind of chain mail, long trousers and boots. Their adversaries were similarly equipped.

142–143. The column of Trajan is a main part of the Forum of Trajan in Rome; its pedestal contained the urn with the ashes of the emperor; the column itself was therefore the emperor's sepulcher. On top formerly stood the gilded statue of the emperor (now replaced by St. Peter). The spiral relief band of the 40 meters high column shows in detail the battles of the Romans with the Dacians (in Rumania), conveying abundant information about the Roman army and army life. It represents, among other things, the emperor addressing the army (page 143), which is gathered around him carrying standards (eagles of the legions). The emperor is surrounded by high-ranking officers. It is characteristic of the late ancient era that the emperor is represented taller than the soldiers. Although the battle scenes on the relief on the front of the famous "Battle Sarcophagus of Ludovisi" are over-crowded, thus confusing the general impression, one fact clearly emerges: the victory of the Romans, the defeat of the enemy. Nowhere is a Roman in serious danger. The general even appears in the center unarmed, but his bearing is triumphant.

144. One of the firmly established concepts of the Roman Empire was the triumph of the general and his army. The Emperor Titus is here represented triumphantly standing on the quadriga. The accompanying lance bearers can only be distinguished by their heads and their spears.

Above: the procession can be seen passing through the wooden triumphal gateway. Placards explain the details of the spoils taken from Jerusalem, the most conspicuous of which is the seven-armed candelabra from the temple of Solomon (Titus had captured Jerusalem in 70 B.C.). The apotheosis of the emperor was depicted on the rich ceiling of the vaulting above the reliefs: an eagle carries the deified emperor towards heaven. The arch of Titus was therefore erected by his successor after the Emperor's death.

145. This relief (large parts of which are in the Cancelleria in the Vatican) originates from the Porta Triumphalis in Rome, as restored under the reign of the Emperor Domitian (81 to 96 A.D.). The panels are in the Vatican, the one depicted here in the Capitol Museum. After Domitian was outlawed through so-called damnatio memoriae, the panels were not destroyed nor was the Emperor's face chiselled off – as was the custom in the circumstances – but the panels were merely removed from the structure and buried. They represented the enthronement of the young prince as successor to his father, Vespasian; Praetorians, members of the imperial bodyguard, armed with long lances and large breastplates, surround the genii of the Roman people, greeting the young Domitian. The reliefs are of the finest quality and are a beautiful example of official Roman art.

BARBARIANS

Pages 146–150

The Greeks considered all non-Greeks, that is, all people not speaking Greek, and most especially the Orientals, as barbarians. The Romans too were considered as barbarians until the time of the emperors, when they ruled Greece and learned to use the language. They were then allowed to partake in the Olympic games – an honor never accorded to barbarians. Naturally the Greeks also considered the natives they found in the country, when they came, to be barbarians, and some Greek tribes, especially the Spartans, held back from intermixing until they perished. On the other hand the autochthones never prevented the Greeks from taking over their useful skilled trades together with their designations. If we examine the Greek language to find foreign constituents and "borrowed words" which were originally not part of the language, but later became indispensable to it, it becomes clear that apart from technical expressions relating to the trades, architecture, and sailing, concepts important for the life of the state and therefore the establishments themselves were taken over from the natives. However intense the differences between the Greeks and natives must have been, the intermixing was equally intense, as is unequivocally shown by the names of the Greek gods alone, of which only Zeus is Greek. The amalgamation of the originally Greek with the originally native elements is so complete, so insoluble, that the constituents of classical Greece, as it appears to us since Homer, can no longer be sorted out. What one understands by Hellenism, that which in spite of servitude and subjugation, which in spite of political decline, has determined the culture of the Occident until today and will continue to be valid in its spiritual power, is the result of the happy penetration of several, today no longer quite clearly discernible elements. On this rests the uniqueness of ancient Greek culture. The Greeks also always attempted to recognize the character, characteristics, and peculiarities of the barbarians; they described their customs and represented them pictorially. There are, for instance, amazingly realistic portraits of Negroes dating back to archaic times. By and large, however, the Greeks only found a deeper understanding of the other nations, with whom they came in contact in war or peace, in the Hellenistic epoch after Alexander the Great. Understandably enough, this contact was mainly established in territories newly opened to Hellenism, especially in the Hellenic provinces of the Orient. The representation of barbarians became a characteristic of artistic activity in the courts of Hellenistic kings and princes, and more especially in the court of Pergamum. In obedience to the Kings of Pergamum several series depicting battles against the Persians and Gauls (pages 146/147) celebrating the victory of the soldiers of Pergamum over the barbarians, and the deliverances of Hellenism, were created and offered as a thanksgiving to the gods, but what really distinguishes these pictures is that not only have the characteristic physical peculiarities of their enemies been faithfully reproduced, but at the same time the world has been handed on a picture of barbarian bravery in the face of death and destruction which can in no way have been inferior to that of the Greeks. It has always been a peculiarly Greek characteristic to accord a certain right even to the enemy in battle. The noblest hero in the Iliad is Hector, the enemy, and the representation of the barbaric Centaurs, the demons of Hellenism, who served as an example of everything non-Greek and barbaric, crowns the south metopes of the Parthenon. Other similar examples could be given, and they are important because they show a distinct contrast between the attitudes of the Greeks and Romans, at least as far as pictorial representations are concerned. The Romans, too, studied the barbarians with whom they came in contact, and who, by now, were neighbors of their ever increasing empire: their knowledge of them was handed down to the world in certain writings. In the pictures of battles fought by Romans against the barbarians, however, only the victories of the Romans are stressed; never was a Roman legionnaire, a Roman knight, or, above all, a general, shown to be in danger of death (see No. 142); to depict a fallen Roman would have been impossible. The Roman was always taught by the state to see in his victories over the enemy tribes only the victory of the righteous cause (in this they were similar to the Orientals), which was blessed by the gods. The conquered barbarians were, of course, gladly taken into, and assimilated by, the Roman army, either singly or as complete contingents, after which, as often happened, they became rightful Roman citizens. Because the Roman emperors were not, and had not been for a long time, Roman born, "barbarians" also attained the throne, non-Romans forced their way into the administration and other offices, and originally foreign religions were tolerated, even encouraged, among them one, which, first mocked and ridiculed, later cruelly persecuted, and finally recognized by the state, conquered not only Rome, not only the Roman empire, but the whole world: Christianity.

EDUCATION

Pages 151–154

Knowledge of the elementary subjects of reading, writing, and simple arithmetic must have been widespread as early as the 6th century B.C. for it was a self-evident prerequisite for the participation in public life which was expected of every citizen: if he was called upon to vote he had to be able to write the name of the person he was voting for on the ballot form. (This was an "ostrakon," a baked potsherd, hence the word ostracism, i.e., banishment as a result of the potsherd ballot,

"Potsherd court"); the accounts of the authorities, which were made public by inscriptions on stone, were displayed in the state market or in the sanctuaries, and were, therefore, accessible to all and supposed to be read. To give one last example: would the many, often very long, inscriptions on vase paintings have been made if a large circle of the buyers had not been able to read? Lessons in reading and writing were therefore a matter of course for many, and not only for the children of the old nobility.

The schoolmaster type has always been in existence, and is the same today as it was (page 151): he sits on an armchair with a cushion; the chair is even standing on a raised podium. The old gentleman is wearing soft leather shoes. The pupils can't be seen, but he is looking at them, with his elbow resting on his hip and his forefinger raised in warning: "Attention."

The Greeks were already writing in 2000 B.C. When the Achaean princes took over the rule of Crete in 1500 B.C. they had the Cretan linear script converted and arranged for the reproduction of Greek sounds. The writings preserved on terra cotta tablets in Crete itself, but also in Mycenae, and above all in old Pylos, Nestor's residence, where many were found, present the oldest stage of the Greek language. After the last invasion of the Greeks into the eastern part of the mediterranean lands, the so-called Doric invasion, during which the Mycenaean strongholds were destroyed, the Greeks abandoned the perfected Mycenaean script and, once more, took over a script form from a "barbarian" nation, the Phoenicians. This was a character script from which even the order and names of the letters were borrowed (probably about 1000 B.C.). Some of the characters of this script differed considerably from tribe to tribe until, finally at the end of the 5th century B.C., the Ionic script became generally used. The Romans took over the script of a Western Greek alphabet and, in turn, reformed it to fit their own sound values, thus creating the Latin script which has since then been generally valid throughout the world. The Gothic script is also an offshoot from it.

The ancients always wrote on stone, bronze, or wooden tablets in the schools, and privately also on folding tablets (diptychon). The writing surfaces were covered with wax which they scratched with a stylus: an ancient writing implement, pointed for writing at one end, and blunted for obliterating at the other. Although Athena is arrayed like a warrior she is writing in her peaceful capacity as Goddess of the Arts and Sciences – Pallas Athena (page 151).

The teaching of the elementary subjects was left to trained teachers and for further education there were philosophical schools and academies which, finally, were not unlike our own high schools and universities. To begin with, lessons were almost certainly on a private basis. Nevertheless, on state orders, lecture and classrooms were soon established in the gymnasiums, buildings which were, anyway, intended for the instruction of youth. The real "education," however, the paedeia, happened, above all, through the contact between the adults and the youth: the contact between the men and the boys and ephebi. Countless Greek pictures tell of this relationship.

When looking at the order of the newly restored columns of the palaestra in Olympia a special characteristic of ancient education can be recognized: the insoluble and matter of course connection between physical and spiritual education and culture. The palaestra consists of a large inner court, surrounded by colonnades. These colonnades lead to rooms, for changing and washing, and for storing clothes and apparatus, but the numerous benches in different rooms make it clear that they were also used as classrooms. There was at all times, therefore, a real harmony of physical and spiritual culture. In the gymnasium in Pergamum, for example, there is a proper lecture room with tiered seats rising in a half circle, as in the theater.

The large Gymnasiums of Roman times also contained a kind of aula, a banqueting hall. This room is usually called the "Emperor's Room," not only because it is larger and loftier and more beautifully decorated than the other rooms, but also because it contains statues of emperors.

151.   The Panaitios painter received his name because on many works attributed to him on stylistic grounds the words "Panaitios is beautiful" were inscribed. Older men, like Aesop (page 106), and Socrates (page 109), liked to carry a gnarled stick with a simple handle, or with a shaped crutch like Priam (page 280), or with no crutch at all like Zeus (page 1) and Priam (page 122), but they were also affected by boys and youths: (pages 265, 267, 249, with round crutch page 264).

Below: Athena with the Attic helmet; she wears the large aegis, with snakes on the hem, like a cloak. The work is by the Triptolemus painter.

152.   The form of this vessel – a cup with a long high handle – is described as kyathos. It is also the work of the Panaitios painter, see page 151. On the book chest, in front of the reading youth, lies a book scroll with the inscription: "The Teachings of Chiron" (an elementary reader). Chiron was a Centaur renowned in legend as the teacher of Achilles, Asclepius and some others.

153.   All kinds of musical implements are hanging on the walls; the cross above the boy with the writing tablet is a tuning key. The seats are mainly simple, four-legged stools with cushions but without backrests (see No. 226, 227). Only the dignified teacher listening to the recitation is distinguished by an armchair.

154.   This is part of a Roman sarcophagus depicting the rearing of the child Dionysus. A young satyr is being beaten by an old Silenus. Perhaps he is being punished for drinking without asking from the leather wine bottle lying in front of him. Leather wine bottles made from animal skins, sewn together, still serve as wine containers in some places today (compare page 265).

SPORTS AND GAMES

Pages 155–183

Daily physical exercise in the gymnasium and palaestra became a habit for Greek boys probably as early as the 6th century B.C. For the men it provided at the same time a welcome opportunity of meeting the youth of the country. The Romans later took over from the Greeks not only the habit of physical exercise, but also the type of building used for it. Beyond doubt the necessity for self assertion in face of the surrounding enemy was the foremost principle in all sporting events, but to be physically fit and always ready in case of war was definitely not the only goal. The purposeful education of the body as well as of the spirit, the close harmony of body and soul, had always been the special educational task of the ancients. Participation in the great games, that were held yearly or every four years in the large festival places, was considered as the crowning reward of the daily exercises. Although many of the sports today seem similar to those of ancient times – running, jumping, discus throwing, wrestling and boxing – they differ in one way: the great sporting festivals of ancient times were always held as festivals in honor of a deity and were in themselves part of a religious ceremony. Religion and physical exercise are so far apart in our conception that to name them in one breath might almost be considered blasphemy. For the Greeks the two went together as a matter of course. The Olympic games were held in the sacred precincts of Zeus in Olympia, the Nemean in Nemea (Zeus), the Isthmian on the isthmus of Corinth (Poseidon) and the Pythian games were held in Delphi (Apollo). These games attained Panhellenic recognition, but there were others of more local significance, for instance in Argos (Hera), in Epidaurus (Asclepius) and above all the Panathenaic festival in Athens, which was held on the feast day of Athena Parthenos. In every case the games were closely connected with the religious festival, with the holy precincts and with the deity itself. Therefore the stadiums lie in closest proximity to the sanctuaries, if they were not, as in early times in Olympia, part of the sanctuaries themselves.

Although a victor of the important games was greatly honored, his achievements were not thought to be entirely due to his own efforts but also to the intervention of the deity itself. The state provided a banquet for him in the Prytaneum, and he was honored and respected by his fellow citizens, but the wreath of twigs from the wild olive trees which the Hellenodike had placed on his head was laid in front of his own native altar: he returned to the deity that which it had given him. Statues of victors were erected in the sanctuaries and lists of their names were guarded in the sacred precincts. The year 776 B.C. stands out, not because it heralded the beginning of the Olympic games, as is often thought, but because from that year on the names of the victors were inscribed on stone tablets and preserved for the world. In connection with these, but as a secondary consideration, a whole system of reckoning time according to the Olympiads was built up, which, of course, attained a general Greek significance reaching far beyond "sport." Consolidated Christendom suspended the games in 394 A.D., and finally severed all connections with the heathen religion, but the Olympic games had by that time completely lost their original significance.

The practice and contest fields provided inspiration for countless Greek paintings and statues. The representation of the "Palaestrites" exercising and competing naked was not an idealized portrayal intended to raise them above everyday life, for it depicted reality. The complete nakedness of male youth on the sports fields of the ancients was taken as a matter of course. Ancient culture, especially Greek culture, was largely determined by men; accordingly women and girls were barred from ancient festivals and were strictly forbidden to enter the stadiums even as onlookers. A unique honor was therefore bestowed on Callipateira, the daughter of Diagoras of Rhodus, when she was allowed to enter the stadium at Olympia contrary to all customs. She attained this honor because she could prove that she came from no ordinary family: her father and three brothers had several times been victors at Olympia – even all together on the same day – and two of her nephews had also been victorious competitors. This happened in the year 450 B.C. and is explained in the scholium to the 7th Olympic Ode by Pindar. The fact that women and girls were not completely barred from sporting activities is shown by the picture of girls swimming, on page 171. Heraea (running contests for women) were also held in Olympia, outside the Olympic games proper; the well-known statue of the woman runner in the Vatican may represent the victorious competitor of such a contest.

155.   The stadium in Delphi lies at the foot of the Phaedriades (page 32), above and in close proximity to the precincts of Apollo. The tiered seats on the mountainside are well preserved up to the curves, but those on the other side have hurled down into the valley. It held about 7000 people.

156.   The columns facing the open courtyard are Doric (in the picture left) and those leading to the various rooms are of the Ionic order. For 30 days before the Olympic games the participants had to train and prepare themselves in the courtyard of the palaestra and in the adjacent gymnasium under the surveillance of the Hellenodike (the director of the games).

Below: The gymnasium in Delphi, a municipal building, lies above the precincts of Athena Pronaia (today called Marmaria). Apart from a running track the gymnasium contains a well preserved walled-in bath basin with steps leading into it, which stands in the hall, as well as special washing places (front right of picture).

157.   Above: A team game with two teams in which a ball that was thrown and had to be caught, and also running, were of importance.

Center: The beginning of a wrestling match in which the contestant on the right is holding the arm of his opponent with both hands; he, in turn, is defending himself by bracing his arm against the shoulder of his antagonist. Beside him a thrower is testing his javelin (see page 159 above) and, on the left, an athlete is getting into position to jump.

Below: Two youths sit opposite one another on the edge of the practice ground. On the left is an ordinary seat without a backrest, on the right a folding seat with animal-like shaped legs (compare pages 171, 192, 288, a Roman folding chair with backrest, page 227). For their own and their friends delight they are setting a dog against a cat; both are held on leads.

158–161.   These pictures which are from the neck of a tapering amphora (the pictures on page 15 right and on page 242 above, stem from the same vessel) represent left: a javelin thrower hurrying to the practice, right: a thrower testing his javelin, and next to him a boy throwing a javelin. By lunging forward the boy gives the javelin its final impetus. The javelin thrower on the bottom, on the other hand, swings it back immediately before throwing it – both types of throw correspond to today's technique. The other pictures depict the procedure of throwing the discus. On page 159 below, a man with a discus is getting ready to throw: he weighs the discus (with an owl on it) in his left hand. On page 159 above he has taken the discus in his right hand and his left is also ready to grasp it, as can be seen from page 160 where the athlete is depicted holding the discus up high with both hands before swinging round, while balancing with his left arm, in preparation for the throw (page 161). The bronze statuette reproduces the archaic presentation of the motif, which Myron classically formulated with his "Discobolus."

162–163.   Prize amphorae are vessels in which the victors of the Panathenaic games in Athens received oil as a prize. These amphorae, which have been in existence since 560 B.C., have a picture of the Goddess Athena throwing a spear, on one side, and a representation of the contest on the other. The one shown on page 162 depicts a boxing match: one man is lying on the floor and signalling with one hand that he is giving up the fight. The boxer on page 163 below, who has been knocked down by a blow to the jaw is also giving the signal of surrender; the referee intervenes with a crack of the whip. Page 163 above shows the attacker with clenched fists and the defendant with open hands. The rules of the contest stipulated that the victor had to go on fighting other challengers. These can be seen on the pictures next to the fight.

164–165.   Either soft or hard bandages were worn for boxing; like the ones the youth on page 164 is binding round his wrist, or like the ones the resting boxer is wearing on page 165 – these have developed into strong straps with a wide hitting surface. The powerful bronze figure from the Thermae Museum is one of the last achievements of Attic art. It is a realistic portrait of a (probably once famous) heavyweight fighter for whom boxing must already have become a kind of profession – how different from the face of the victorious boxer on page 175.

It is characteristic of Greek art that what the painters saw in the Palaestra they used, without any more ado, for their representations of mythical battles. On page 164 below, a Lapith is punching a Centaur with a straight left to the head, and is ready, as in a boxing match, to follow on with his right. The wrestler's grip on page 167 is represented in the same spirit, by the same painter: the painter of the Florentine Centaur battles.

166–167. These pictures represent the progession of a wrestling match. The contestants attempt to get a grip on each other's hands (page 166 above), one antagonist has gripped the hand of the other (page 167 center), now one of them has quickly turned around, he swings his opponent over his shoulder (page 166 below) and lays him "on the mat." Naturally the fights in the great games were divided into age groups, although the pictures often show bearded men fighting young boys but this is only to be expected when one considers the customary companionship offered to youth by the adults.

168–169. Running was divided into short and long-distance running as it is today. The picture on page 168 above (from a prize amphora) shows the long-distance runners, close together, approaching the finishing point with long strides. A special kind of running contest was the torch race (page 168 below), in which a flaming torch had to be brought to the altar, where the priest awaited the victor. Another special kind of contest was the weapon race (generally shield and helmet), which has a direct bearing on the necessities of war. The famous bronze statuette in Tübingen, reproduced here on page 169, shows the runner with outstretched right arm and bent knees (first stage of the low starting position, which was then unknown), tensely awaiting the signal to be off (today the plume is missing from the helmet and the shield from the arm). This outstanding work is reminiscent of the statue of the armed runner Epicharinus, which was erected in the Acropolis soon after the Persian wars (490 to 479 B.C.).

170. An indoor swimming pool is indicated by the Doric column. One girl is swimming, another is oiling herself, and a third is jumping from the small board in the center; all the girls are naked. The work is by the Andokides painter, who from 530 B.C. worked on red-figure painting which was then beginning in Athens.

Below: Chariot races were considered to be among the noblest contests in the great games. The chariot is pulled by four horses (see pages 134–135) and driven by the charioteer (see page 174).

171. To make the activities of Greek youth on the practice grounds come to life, or to see a Palaestra rise from today's ruins, one has only to look at the pictures on innumerable Greek vases. They are most beautiful to see.

Above: Two tall boys are clearing the dust of the Palaestra off themselves with scraping irons (this slight motif from everyday life is rendered monumental by the famous "Apoxyomenos" by Lysippus). Several oil containers, like the one the girl after her bath, (page 170 above) and the boy below, are using, can be seen hanging up in the interior picture of the vessel. The scene below left is usually interpreted to mean that a servant boy is taking a thorn out of a boy's foot. Nothing of this is to be seen however and the movements indicate a foot massage. The clothes have been put on a folding stool (see page 157).

172–173. The palaestrites in ancient times always concerned themselves with the maintenance and preparation of their playing fields. A hoe which was used among other things for loosening the soil of the jumping pit is often shown in the pictures (pages 158–159). The picture inside the bowl by the Panaitios painter shows how it was done (page 142 above): loose soil as well as grass is being packed into a wicker basket (compare with a similar basket at the grape harvest page 206). That the work is being done by an athlete and not by a youthful groundsman is shown by the headgear which is worn by athletes on other sports pictures.

Below: The victors of sporting contests were always feted and honored. The victor of a javelin throwing contest, a boy garlanded with a wreath, is standing on the podium. In front of him stands the judge. In the picture next to it (page 173) the judge is decorating him with the sashes, chains, and garlands which are the victor's due.

174–175. One of the most beautiful statues of victors which has been preserved for us is the famous charioteer in Delphi. He was originally represented holding the reins in the chariot, with the horses in front of him, but only a few remains of these were found. The bronze head of the bearded man, on page 175, shows the flat nose of a boxer. Satyros was nine times victor in the boxing ring: five times in Nemea, twice in Delphi and twice in Olympia. He was, therefore, in "top form" for at least 16 years and until a comparatively advanced age. The head is by Silanios who also created the head of Plato.

176. The reproduction of the blunt face of a boy from the lower classes is characteristic of the Hellenistic epoch, which searched for new motifs and aspects in art. The situation in which the young rider was represented is not clear to us. Perhaps he was jumping over an obstacle. It was found together with the bronze head of Zeus (page 2), in the sea by Cape Artemisium (Euboea).

177. The pancratium combined boxing and wrestling – beating, pushing, and even biting were allowed. The ring on the head of the statuette is for hanging up; the statuette also served as a weight.

178. This picture stems from the grave of Panaitios which was found in the cemetery on the Eridanus in front of the Dipylon in Athens. The picture, which probably shows the deceased as a child, is taken from the lekythos which was originally in the left hand corner of the relief; this vessel played an important part in the cult of the dead, especially during the 5th century B.C. (see page 301).

179. This relief, like the one on page 157, stems from a statue base which was buried during the hurried erection of the Themistoclean wall in 478 B.C.

180. The man sitting on the folding stool (like the one on page 157) is throwing a ball which the boys riding on men's shoulders are supposed to catch.
Below: A kind of blind man's buff (ephedrismos) is here depicted by the Swallow painter.

181. Girls on swings are known to us already from Crete from the 2nd millennium B.C. Swinging almost had a religious significance. The picture on the other side of the vessel from which this one is taken is connected with the Anthesteria feast, a death festival held in spring. The satyr who is pushing the swing also belongs to the religious sphere. The swing consists of ropes fastened to an ordinary four-legged stool.
Below: The terra cotta spinning tops found in children's graves show that this game was a favorite pastime enjoyed also by grown ups, as it is today.

182. The Greeks and Romans always used sheep's knuckle bones (astragaloi) for playing dice. The sides were distinguished by markings comparable to our own. The figure of the young girl lost in her dreams and throwing dice is not a straightforward copy of a Greek original for the head has been clearly remodeled as a portrait. It may have been the monument of a girl who died in her youth.
Below: Compare the boy's fur cap with the one on page 241.

183. The kottaboss game was a favorite pastime at a symposium. It was also played by young girls who liked to treat it as a love oracle (page 263). The game is played by throwing the last drops from a drinking cup onto a plate which is placed high on a pole, so that it falls with a bang onto a second plate underneath. Here a boy is leaning against a pillar (such as is often used in the palaestra for hanging up clothes, see page 171) and watching a young girl, richly ornamented with rings on her arms and legs, performing acrobatic feats. She is standing on her hands and her feet are touching the lower plate of a kottaboss stand. The girl is dressed in a short jerkin similar to our bathing costumes.

HUNTING

Pages 184–187

Artemis was for the Greeks, as Diana was for the Romans, the protectress of the animals and of all living creatures. She was the mistress of the wind-swept mountain heights and she was the Goddess of the Hunt. As Goddess of the Hunt she is praised and lauded in the Homeric Hymns. She kills the animals with arrows shot from her golden bow, and the stags in the mountains with a spear (page 186). Homeric accounts and allegories speak – as does the conception of the goddess herself – of the knowledge of the Greeks about the practices and necessities, as well as the customs, of the hunt. Whether they actually hunted lions or only knew the hunt from mythical and pictorial traditions must remain problematical. Their own hunting grounds certainly provided enough opportunities for them to hunt wild boar, stags, deer, hares, birds and fish, while the Romans, going further afield in their provinces also hunted and caught bears (page 186), as well as lions and the fleet-footed gazelles. Lions, stags and wild boar most often appear in the Greek representations of mythical hunts: so Heracles strangles the lion of Nemea, captures the Cerynitic hind and the Crommyonian sow. The hunt of the Calydonian boar, which had devastated the land, became a meeting of the noblest heroic characters. Meleager was in the forefront, and the presence of Atalanta proves that, in early times, noblewomen participated in the hunts. This is already shown by the Mycenaean wall frescoes in the palace of Tiryns. Nothing is known of women hunting from later times.

184.   The hydria belongs to a group of vases of which about twenty were found in Caere only. They are therefore often held to be the products of an Etruscan workshop, although certain stylistic peculiarities, as well as the Ionic inscription on the piece in the Louvre, seem to imply that they are the work of an Ionian who became domiciled in Etruria.

Below: The man on the wild boar hunt – not necessarily Meleager – carries a hunting club but he gives the final blow with his sword. The rocks on the side indicate the gorge in which the boar was trapped.

185.   Eos, the goddess of the dawn, was enamored of the young hunters Tithonus and Cephalus, one of whom is probably here depicted. The hunter wears shoes and laced gaiters, a chiton, a short cloak and a soft hat with a wide brim (see No. 128). He carries a hunting club, two spears, and a sword in the scabbard on his belt. He is accompanied by a nice hound.

186.   This Roman sarcophagus is one of a group which repeatedly represents real and mythical hunts. On the left, a huntsman with a short hunting spear attacks a boar, which has been trapped by two dogs. In the center, the master of the hunt, seated on a horse, is being greeted by a hunting companion. His triumphant bearing is reminiscent of the general's on the Ludovisi battle sarcophagus (page 142). On the right, stags are being driven into net traps. Among the hunters, the rider on the right is distinguished by a hood, the others wear shoes and a short cloak like the Greek huntsmen but long trousers and a jerkin with sleeves have been added. The live chained bear lying on his back on a two-wheeled ox cart was probably destined for the circus (see pages 70–71).

187.   It was not uncommon for the Greeks and Romans to breed and train dogs for the hunt.

Below: The breed of the dog licking himself is similar to that of the dog on page 185. The picture stems from a representation of the dying Adonis who was killed by a wild boar while hunting.

XLII

Even if the word "banausos," as used in some modern languages, has changed its original Greek meaning, the contempt it implies has been handed down from the ancients. Today the word describes a narrow-minded, low-thinking person without intellectual interests, but the Greeks applied it to all those who earned their livelihood by working with their hands. They included all the artisans, as well as those active in trade and commerce. These were not merely the slaves but represented a large part of the population, yet they enjoyed no particular esteem, not even when their work made them rich. Although under the peak of the Greek democracy they were given access to the national assemblies, and therefore to the offices, it is doubtful whether they rose in esteem. Conditions under the Romans were not very different, yet Pericles was on friendly terms with a man whose fame was widespread in his own time and has endured until today – Phidias. If the face on the first south metope of the Parthenon is his self portrait (page 107), he cannot be regarded as a low-minded, narrow-thinking, person, neither can the craftsmen, potters and vase painters who in their time created works of timeless value. Certainly what they created was intended only for their own time, for immediate use in the house or cemetery and for export. They were, therefore, artisans also in our sense of the word, but their products in no way appertained to the modern meaning of the word "banausos."

As in most countries in the middle ages, the artisans lived in professional groups in certain streets and quarters, and in Athens today many still live in the same areas as in ancient times. Thus the potter's quarter, the Kerameikos, lay close to the agora (state market). It was the same everywhere else, in Corinth and in all the places of the ancient world.

188.   This small, terra cotta tablet was found, together with many others, in a Poseidon sanctuary near Corinth. The holes in the middle or top served to hang it on a tree or to fasten it to a building. A man is hacking the soil, a boy is collecting it in a wicker basket, and another man pushes the clay, the raw material of the potters, to the surface. A water jug (amphora) is hanging down into the ditch on a rope so that the workers can quench their thirst.

Below: Athena, protectress of artisans and especially of the potters and artists working in metal, is wearing a helmet and a chiton covered by a cloak which she has wound round her hips like an apron. This is the typical working garment of the professional artisan. The horse she is modeling is not quite finished, one leg is still missing. Lumps of clay lie in front of the pedestal, and above left are implements for measuring, boring and sawing. It is the work of the Pan painter (compare page 185).

189.   Pinaces (as on page 188 above) are hanging up next to the furnace. All kinds of implements are lying about: a saw, a small hammer, a strigilis and aryballos: Above are two feet belonging to a figure. The statue of the boy (reminiscent of the "Praying Boy" in Berlin) is lying on the floor, the head is still lying beside it. The larger than life figure of a warrior, like the one on page 136, is standing under a frame. Two workmen are wearing artisan's aprons; the one sitting by the fire is wearing a protective cap like Hephaestus-Vulcanus on page 190.

190.   The Cyclopes are renowned as the helpers of Vulcan.

Below: The man painting the statue is being watched in his work by Zeus, Nike and Heracles himself, whose image is receiving the last refinements. The craftsman wearing apron and cap is applying color with a stylus from a small bowl which a serving companion is heating up for him on the left. This process is called encaustic and the man is an "encaustes agalmaton."

191.   An assistant is beating, with delicate instruments, a greave for a leg, on a small anvil which is standing on a block. On the right, only partly seen, stands Hephaestus. He is holding a small hammer, like the one that was recently found in the workshop of Pheidias in Olympia.

192.   The activity in the butcher's shop on the right has been clearly depicted in the slight but vivid style of painting peculiar to Boeotic workshops. The two columns indicate a covered place.

Below: The cobbler's worktable has three legs, the implements are on a ledge above. The artisan is distinct from the boy's father, an eminent customer, because of his characteristic apron. The branches on both their heads lift the otherwise realistic picture out of the sphere of ordinary life.

193.   A woman has come into the oil merchant's shop. He has taken the oil from an oil jug (a pelike like the vessel itself) helped by a small assistant.

Below: From this and one similar picture, the painter received the name Pig painter. Apart from pigs the merchant has all kinds of other things to sell, which are stored in the baskets.

194.   The counter is protected by a roof.

Below: A cobbler is at work on the left; two pairs of lasts stand on the cupboard in front of him. On the right a man is spinning: he is pulling a thread from a ball and winding it around a kind of spindle. The relief stems from a sarcophagus with a Greek inscription in Ostia.

195.   This relief depicts the inside of a shop. Above the ground floor is a second story with windows overlooking the street. The customers are sitting on stools, while the shopkeeper is having a large cloth spread out before them.

Below: This picture shows a whole store of metal implements like tongs, knives, graters, a saw and a plane. The relief is from a tomb in Porto di Roma.

196.   This floor mosaic served as a kind of company coat of arms in front of the office of a trading firm dealing in the exchange of goods. The picture shows Amphorae containing wine or oil being transferred from one ship to another.

Below: The men are carrying heavy low wicker baskets which are covered and tied up with cords. Calpurnius was an argentarius – a money exchanger and banker.

197.   This part of a significant relief from a tomb of Flavian times represents a family or tribal tomb. On the outer wall on the right of the picture, are, among other things, busts in full relief like the ones from the family tomb on page 300. On the roof there is a sofa, like the one on page 223 below. The purpose of the machine is not completely clear. It is a crane-like implement for lifting heavy loads and is worked by a flywheel. The high mast is secured by several lines.

198.   The size and number of corn mills indicate an extensive business. The pictures show that bakers were also millers.

199–202.   The Greek, and later Roman, coins, were stamped and not cast as they are today. The under stamp was placed on a small anvil and the planchet (a plain disk of metal) was laid on top of it and beaten with the top stamp. Many coins still show the straining apart of the metal, e.g., page 201 below left. The Greeks liked to choose the chief deities of the cities in question to be represented on the coins (page 199–200). Alexander's successors, the Diadochs and other Hellenistic princes, had their own portraits stamped on one side and the image of a deity, or a religious symbol with an inscription, on the reverse (page 201 below). This portrait stamping was taken over by the Romans (page 202 above). The earliest Roman coins were cast, heavy, thick, and peculiarly difficult to handle. They were made of so-called aes grave – heavy ore – (page 202 below). The Greek coins, especially those dating back to archaic and classical times, are distinguished by their outstanding beauty (page

199. The coins reproduced on pages 200–202 are examples from the coin collection of the archaeological institute of Giessen university and are at present kept in the university library.

203–204. The ships are in the harbor of Ostia; the lighthouse can be seen in the middle above. The harbor of Ostia also appears to be represented in the rich relief on page 204: in the center is the three-storied lighthouse with an enormous flame, above it an emperor's statue, on the right of that a triumphal arch with an elephant quadriga, on the left edge the goddess of the town (Tyche – Fortuna); on the right the youthful Bacchus, and below him wine amphorae are being unloaded along a gangway. A large sailing ship on the left is coming into harbor. The letters VL on the sail have been interpreted as votum libero "Consecrated to Liber."

COUNTRY LIFE

Pages 205–209

205. This method of carrying animals, the calf carried on the shoulders, has been the custom of herdsmen and peasants since time immemorial. Christianity also took over the pictorial image of the "good shepherd" with his lamb. This work by an important Attic master expressively shows the contrast between the dumb animal and the alert bearded man.

206. An enormous vine spreads its branches from the center all over the surface of the picture, almost like a tree. It is so strong that small grape pickers can sit and stand on its branches. The harvest is being gathered into a wicker basket on the right, and into a large earthenware barrel on the left. Below: The men are wearing leather aprons; a boy gathers the beaten down fruit into a basket with a handle. It is the work of the Antimenes painter.

207. The fruit is brought in a large "krater," emptied into barrels and pressed by foot. Below: The peasant plowing is wearing an ordinary plate-shaped hat. The small figure of Minerva was originally not part of the group.

208. The armed attendants of Heracles are driving away a herd of cattle belonging to Geryones, the three-bodied monster whom Heracles destroyed (this is depicted on the reverse side of the vessel). Some of the animals have beautifully plaited tails. Below: The herdsman is sitting in front of a stone house with arched entrances. He is working on a branch, with a bent knife; behind him is a watchdog. A goat is milked (below left) from behind, not obliquely from the front as today.

209. The large mosaic from the Fortuna sanctuary in Palestrina has had many adventures and travelled far before reaching the courtyard of the Diocletian thermae (Thermae Museum), where it is at present. It has been often and extensively restored, and some of the details may have been distorted, but the general effect of the composition and the themes illustrating life on the Nile during the time of the fruitful flood correspond to the antique condition. The mosaic, judged by its forms and perspective, has been placed in the time of Septimus Severus (193–211 A.D.). Below: Here is an idyllic country scene in which goats graze by the water and in the lovely hills surrounding a small sanctuary (in the background on the right), which is marked by the sitting goddess in front of it and by the altar adorned with creepers (compare page 51).

CARRIAGES

Pages 210–211

210. This is actually a representation of the journey of the deceased to the other side, and the boy in front may be taken to be the guide; yet the horses, the carriage, the lady with the parasol and, in fact, all the details recreate the habits of everyday life.

Below: The picture shows a four-wheeled carriage with winged sides. The man, driven by his coachman, is inspecting his lands. The coachman holds the whip in his right hand; a dog is accompanying them.

211. The post carriage drawn by four horses was of great importance in the Roman empire. It is a solid, four-wheeled carriage with a superstructure covered by an awning. The travellers can be seen through an opening in the front. The coachman is holding the customary whip in his left hand.

Below: This part of a relief clearly shows the beautiful leatherwork of the harness. The lion's head between the pole horses is the shaft head.

HOUSES AND COURTYARDS

Pages 212–221

The "turning inwards" is the main characteristic of the Greek as well as of the Roman dwelling house. The house has no outer façade and as light and air enter from the inside, often not even windows. A narrow entrance, the prothyron, leads from the street to the interior. The interior is the center of the house and all the necessary rooms like dining room, bedrooms, kitchen, storeroom, etc. lead off from it. The Greek interior is an open courtyard which in wealthy houses is surrounded by a colonnade (peristyle). The center of the Roman house, on the other hand, is the atrium (page 212) – this arrangement, like the word itself, is of Etruscan origin. It is an enclosed, covered space with a small opening (impluvium) in the roof and a depression in the floor for the collection and disposal of rainwater. The ancestral portraits of the Romans stood in the atrium. The low doors in the walls lead to the alae (narrow wings) and to the adjoining rooms. A large main door opens into the triclinium (page 214), the dining room. The Greek peristyle began to be built on to Roman houses already during, but more especially after, the republican era. The peristyles are widened and enlarged into great courtyards with gardens (page 213), like the ones in the palaces of the kings of Pergamum. Pillars with arches are used instead of columns, thus forming an arcade. The Romans also developed multi-storied architecture, already begun by the Greeks, and added a second story with an arcade to the inner courtyards. This method, developed by the Romans, has been used in the middle ages and in modern times to build façades around courtyards, which count among the finest examples of European architecture. In the big cities, especially in Rome, there were, apart from these inward-facing houses, large houses with several stories and without courtyards – like tenement houses.

We know many examples of Greek dwelling house architecture from Priene, Miletus, Pergamum, and above all from the island of Delos where, apart from the sanctuaries and shops, a whole town was excavated. Recently remains have also been discovered of Olynthus in Northern Greece (Chalcidice). They consist of floors and walls, which the Romans also took over from the Greeks and developed to suit their own requirements. All Greek flooring was finished with fine mosaic. In Olynthus they are two-toned and consist of light and dark pebbles (page 216), but in Pergamum and on the island of Delos colored mosaics have been found (pages 218–219). The walls were covered with Ogygian stucco and painted. The Romans, in various periods, often widened narrow rooms with illusionary painting (page 220) for example: colonnades throwing shadows, and other representations of perspective. They often even negated the enclosing character of a room by covering it with paintings representing panoramas of gardens, towns, and landscapes. Some exquisitely beautiful stuccoes produce the same results.

In spite of their preference for life in the open, in the market places and in the public rooms, the ancients developed a high standard of housing which can hardly have been inferior to our own today.

214. The ancients did not sit at the table to eat their meals but reclined on a couch (see page 262). These were generally arranged in a horseshoe shape, leaving room for free access in front. In Pompeii they were built of stone and covers and cushions were used to make them comfortable. The food and drink were placed in front of the couches and the area beyond was used by the servants, musicians, and dancing girls.

215. Nearly every Roman house had a lararium where the gods of the home were venerated. The one shown here has been made into a small chapel: a short colonnade on a solid base.

216. Pegasus, the winged horse, is the son of Medusa and Poseidon. Only Bellerophon managed to tame him, by the Corinthian spring Pirene (see page 95). Riding on Pegasus he killed Chimaera, a monster from Lycia with a lion's body, a snake's tail and a goat's head.

217. The card bearing the artist's signature is represented in the mosaic, as though it were stuck on with sealing wax, and one corner was coming away.

218. The peristyle mosaic is edged with a spiral pattern similar to the one on a correspondingly placed mosaic in a house in Pompeii. The one shown here is a so-called "swastika meander."

219. The crouching dog is intended as a warning to visitors, corresponding to our inscription: Beware of the dog. Already in Pompeii then, dogs were used to guard the house.

220. The socle is painted with columns standing in front of a wall and with a frieze of landscapes above.

221. The stucco reliefs which covered the vaulted ceiling of a Roman house in front of the Farnesina in Rome belong to the great achievements of decorative art in Roman times. A landscape with figures is sketched in a few light strokes.

DOMESTIC LIFE

Pages 222–232

The following pictures show the inner life of the house, which was usually withdrawn from the public gaze. The bridal state, weddings and marriage (pages 222–223), as well as the fervently entreated blessing of children, have always inspired artists, with most varying results (pages 224 and 225, compare also the children in the Ages of Man pages 268–271). The pictures also give an often surprisingly clear and detailed description of the furnishings and inner decorations of the houses (pages 226–227). The pictures, as well as the utensils which they depict, most lovingly reveal small intimacies and secrets of the toilet (pages 230–232).

222. The woman next to the bride, who is sitting and gazing thoughtfully in front of her, is placing a wreath upon her head. The picture depicts the last moments before the wedding ceremony. Eros, the God of Love, brings wreaths of myrrh. On the left, a girl in a peplos is bringing a chest.

Below right: The veiled bride, already married, is about to leave her parents' house and to go to the house of her husband. Both pictures stem from a "lutrophorus," the vessel in which the water for the ceremonial bridal bath was carried. It was the custom to bury these vessels with girls who died unmarried, so that the next world would grant them the wedding and marriage which this world had denied.

223. An Etruscan married couple are happily and peacefully lying together on the kline eating a meal. This is in contrast to the Greek custom which decreed that the men ate their festive meals in the company of hetaerai, but not of their wives.

Below: A Roman married couple sit in a tender embrace on a piece of furniture, which, with its turned legs, wide frame, and arm and back rests, corresponds exactly to the sofa of today (compare also page 197). A small dog is on the left.

225. The relief depicts several scenes side by side: on the left and on the right the parents are going out with their child in a four-wheeled carriage, in the center scene, a boy is playing with a goose (see page 240) and beside it with a "scooter," which was probably a preparation for learning to walk. The same boy is depicted in all four scenes and must have been the boy in the small coffin.

226–227. Greek and Roman furniture was made mainly of wood and was partly ornamented with metal. The basic forms of the seating arrangements developed in the 6th and 5th century B.C., from the simple stool (page 122) to the richly ornamented throne (pages 43, 65, 71), have, apart from minor modifications, remained the same throughout the ages. There was the simple stool without arm or back rests, with four vertical legs and a horizontal seat usually covered by a cushion (pages 152, 153, 192, 222, 248, 273, 279). Then there was the favorite folding stool with movable legs which were mainly carved to look like animal legs (pages 141, 180, 192, 288). The doctor's chair on page 227 has the same crossed legs, but these are no longer movable. It also has material-covered armrests leading to a high back rest, thus making a comfortable, throne-like, chair which was particularly popular in Roman times (compare page 289). The cobbler's stool on page 194 is simply made of joined laths. One of the most beautiful pieces of furniture is the elastically curved classical chair, with its curved legs and rounded back ending in a broad, flat surface (pages 153, 226, 233, 243, 248, 250, 251, 253, 269, 278, 300). The Exekias Pinax on page 288 shows the earlier form of the 6th century, with a shorter back-rest ending in a curved-down swan's neck and head. The most beautiful example of a classical chair is on the tombstone of Hegeso, page 298.

The kline served as a sleeping couch (page 226 below), an eating couch (pages 262, 264, 269), as a side bed (page 285) and as a deathbed (page 288). The head of the kline is built up (page 262, 289) or raised through a high elaborate leg. The kline is covered by a thick mattress which hangs down over both ends (page 262) and by a narrow cloth. Cushions were placed at the head when required to give support to the upper part of the body (page 262). The kline of Danae (page 226), who was awaiting the golden shower of Zeus, is covered by a richly embroidered cloth hanging down to the ground. Tables, usually with three legs, were placed in front of the kline during mealtimes (pages 252, 262, 264).

On page 227 a doctor is reading a book scroll: he is studying a medical book and sitting in front of the opened medicine cupboard. Above it is the open case with his surgical instruments (compare with the cupboard in the cobbler's workshop on page 194). The girl on page 227 is hurrying towards a door with a key in her hand. This door, like most of them were, is made of wood. Bronze nail heads can be seen on the cross beams (other doors on pages 64, 70, 71). The girl is carrying a small chest, such as is often seen in women's closets (pages 222, 233, 248). They were used to keep small articles of value, jewelry etc., and were also used by the boys for their books (page 152). The old man from the phlyacography burlesque on page 65 has a large, not easily movable, wooden chest – a money chest for a respectable fortune.

228–229.   Great stress has always been laid on providing the household with water. The Romans spared no effort in bringing large quantities of water to the towns from afar, through their aqueducts (page 94). Polycrates, or Peisistratus, the tyrant of Athens, also considered underground water supply systems to be of special importance, and the kings of Pergamum even managed to install a high pressure water system. The water from ordinary springs was harnessed in earliest times. Pipes were laid from which the water flowed into the basins or into the vessels in which it was carried, through a lion's head (page 229). Well houses were also developed (page 229, compare with the Pirene in Corinth page 95). The hydria was the vessel used for carrying water. It has two handles for lifting it up and one vertical one for carrying (pages 229, 168, 247). From deep wells or cisterns (page 89) the water was hauled up by ropes and pulleys, or with the help of a special drawn bucket arrangement (page 228 below) which is still used in some places today. The fetching and carrying of water in ancient times was generally left to the women and girls. Hence the numerous portrayals of girls at the wells and the reason why men have always used this opportunity to approach the water-bearers (pages 288–289).

230.   Bathing tubs were, of course, known by both Greeks and Romans. The Greeks took over the arrangement from the Cretans, as well as the word, for "Asaminthos" has pre-Greek origins. The pictures also repeatedly show the smaller washbasin on a high pedestal, which was used equally by boys and girls. It was also to be found in the sports practice institutions: The boy is holding a strigilis (see page 171), and above the washbasin there is a bundle consisting of a sponge and oil flask, which the boys and young men always took with them to the Palaestra (compare with page 226 – the same bundle with an added net – and pages 152, 159, 171, 172, 189, 277).

231–232.   The girl crouching in the bath was used as an artistic motif as early as the 5th century B. C., before it attained monumental representation in Hellenistic times (page 17). It is always characteristic of the Greeks that motifs based on the intimate observation of everyday life are transformed and used in the representation and characterization of the deities, especially Aphrodite. A Homeric hymn already gives a detailed and unrestrained description of the goddess in her bath: how she cleans and anoints herself and combs her hair (compare page 279), before meeting her lover Anchises. Pictures like the one on the charming acorn lekythos from Berlin may be unmythically interpreted even though Eros is helping the girl to wash her hair. What other purpose did the bath serve than to please the lover? Who was better qualified to assist in such an undertaking than the little God of Love? Mirrors are important toilet requisites among the women, but men are never shown with one. They were mainly small table mirrors (page 231) with handles in the form of statuettes. The outside is decorated and the inside mirror surface smoothly polished. The material was bronze or silver. Page 232 shows the mirror being used after the bath, Eros sits on the edge of the tub. Two women (nymphs) on a rocky seat are finely engraved on the outer side of the mirror on page 232. The one on the left is holding an alabastron (perfume vessel) in one hand and with the other she is holding a mirror for her companion who is straightening her hair with both hands.

COSTUME

Pages 233–246

The main features of Greek and Roman costume are basically similar, despite minor individual differences. The Greek chiton corresponds to the Roman tunica in the same way as the Greek himation (cloak) corresponds to the Roman toga. Ancient costume consisted of only a few individual garments. There were fashionable styles, like the high waist for women after the 4th century B.C., but clothes were never subjected to the continually changing dictates of fashion.

Two-piece clothing like shirt and blouse, or jacket and trousers, was unknown to both Greeks and Romans. Chiton and tunica varied in length according to the purpose for which they were used, but the one-piece effect was always retained. The Greeks considered long trousers to be barbaric because they were worn by the Persians, so whenever men or women are depicted wearing trousers they are either Persians or Amazons (page 130), or archers in Persian costume (compare, however, with the costume of the burlesque actor on pages 65–67). The Romans also disdained to wear trousers but nevertheless recognized their value during winter campaigns, so that they were intro- duced into isolated army contingents. In this the Romans were probably also following the custom of the Gauls and Teutons, with whom they were fighting and in whose cold territories they were forced to be (pages 140–143). The auriga (charioteer) also wore a garment with sleeves and trousers (page 75). The chiton, like the tunica (pages 56, 195, 244), is a shirt garment, sewn on only one side (page 8) and generally with sleeves which could be fastened or buttoned (pages 16, 279). It is made of thin material which often clings to the body. Painters like to represent it so thin that the shape and features of the body become visible underneath (pages 233, 264). The sleeves are short and narrow (page 16), or trailing (pages 19, 105, 248, 250, 264), according to the material. Servants usually wore long sleeves down to the wrists (pages 296, 298). The garment, especially in classical times, was enriched by one or sometimes two girdles around the hips, over which the material was pouched. The men's chiton hardly differed from the women's and could also be worn with wide sleeves (e. g. pages 14, 19), but is hardly ever to be seen with more than one girdle. The single girdle, on the other hand, was quite commonly used, especially with a short chiton like the one worn by Hephaestus, the smith (pages 14, 190), or by the warrior (pages 128, 278), the hunter (page 185), the rider Leagros (page 242) and the small servant (page 295), as well as by the men for whom a large garment was a hindrance in their work. The short chiton, the chitoniskos, was also worn by the hoplites, under their armor, e. g. pages 122–127, page 251 (Amazons). Embroidered or woven patterns were very popular (pages 128, 280). The long ornamented man's chiton was the priest's robe of office (pages 44, 168) as well as that of the cithara player (page 249). The charioteers are also always to be seen wearing the long garment (pages 134, 170, 174).

The cloak (himation) was an important piece of clothing worn in various sizes either directly over the naked body or over a chiton, in which way it was also worn by the men. Zeus wears his large cloak so that the upper right part of his body remains free (page 1), so do Demosthenes (page 111) and the referees (pages 162–163, 172–173), the master brass founders (page 189) and the men lamenting the dead (page 287). The cloak was therefore worn like this mainly for dignified occa- sions (compare also with the Roman style page 145), and in a similar way, of course, by boys at school and at play (pages 152, 154). The cloak is a large rectangular piece of cloth. It could also be used to cover the whole body, as is shown by the dignified figure of Sophocles (page 107, philos- opher page 110. For large cloaks worn over a chiton see pages 15, 19, 105, 193, 276). Small cloaks were also used and were worn like shawls around the shoulders and arms (page 267), and the chlamys (Chlamydion) with the pointed ends falling back and front was secured or buttoned on one shoulder (e. g. pages 23, 181, 184, 185, 192). The tunica is the usual Roman undergarment which was covered on festive occasions by the toga (e. g. pages 46, 52–55, 235, 236). The attend- ants of the sacrifice (Camilli) wear the tunic without a toga (pages 56, 244). Greek priests officiated at sacrificial ceremonies with uncovered heads, while to cover the head with the toga was part of Roman sacrificial law (pages 52–55). Greek women veiled their heads if they were priestesses (page 47), when they entered a sanctuary (page 43), or even on their way to it (page 234), when a sacrifice was offered at the grave (pages 50, 302), at weddings (page 222), and the central figure on the Exekias Pinax (page 285), the chief mourner is also veiled as are some of the women depicted on tomb reliefs to represent the dead (pages 269, 274, 298). The peplos is a Doric garment, in contrast to the Ionic chiton. It is a simple rectangular piece of cloth which was wrapped around the body so that one side remained open (this side was called phainomeris, leg-showing side). It was fastened on one shoulder with pins and could be enriched by a fold (apoptygma), a pouch (Kolpos), as well as by girdles (pages 47, 280 – fold without girdle; pages 7, 190 – fold with single girdle; page 285 below – girdle with drawn-over pouch).

Generally Greeks, as well as Romans, went bareheaded into the street, the market, the senate etc. but special headgear (hoods, caps and hats) was worn on special occasions. The artisan at work wore a simple, pointed, leather cap (pages 189, 190), similar to the ones worn by herdsmen and peasants (pages 193, 241, with a brim, page 45). The same sort of hat was also worn by travellers, such as the soldier (page 69), the Dioscuri, who were always on the move (page 221), and Orestes and Phylades who reached Agamemnon's grave after long wanderings. Herdsmen in cold districts sometimes also needed a fur hat (pages 182, 241). The wide-brimmed hat worn by the Etruscan peasant on page 201 is more like the other kind of travelling hat, which consists of a convex crown and a wide vertical brim which was sometimes a little turned up. It is characteristic of Hermes, the messenger of the gods (pages 11, 27), but was also worn by hunters (pages 184–185) and riders (page 216). The latter sometimes wore it with the crown shaped to a point like the riders on page 131, or Leagros on horseback on page 242.

Women are usually to be seen only with bands in their hair which were tied into a bow (compare with the hair bands worn by the men at the symposium), or with a cap which is skillfully wound from a wide band knotted on the forehead so that the top of the head is covered (page 243). The pictures show the numerous possibilities of this slight article of clothing. The flat plate-like hat with a point in the middle, as worn by the girl with the heart-shaped fan on page 232, originated in the 4th century B.C. The girl is probably on her way to a sanctuary, like the family on the votive relief on page 43.

The representation of people going barefoot does not necessarily imply a reproduction of ancient realities, for it often corresponds to the intention of raising the depicted person to a higher sphere above the realities of everyday life. Augustus, for instance, is shown in full armor but without footwear (statue at the Primaporta page 116). It is therefore more significant that footwear is sometimes shown – just because it was worn (even if going barefoot was more usual then, than it is today).

A simple sandal consisting of a firm sole and straps around the instep, heel, and ankle, was most commonly worn (page 123). On reliefs only the soles are often indicated by the artists, the shoes were painted on: (e. g. pages 12, 47, 50, 269, 276, 282, 298 – all these must be imagined, like the woman's sandals on page 278). The sole was doubled and raised for the cothurnus of the actors (page 65). How this sandal was put on and laced is shown by the naked girl after her bath on page 245; she twists the ends together with both hands.

Socrates on page 109 wears very simple sandals, as does Achilles on page 123. The sandals of the gods (pages 10, 18) were more richly plaited and ornamented. The construction of the strapwork, the lacing, and the pointed ends of the laces are clearly reproduced on the relief in Rome (page 145). The shoes of a Praetorian are shown in detail on page 245. Sometimes the lacing stretches to the middle of the calf (page 22). The sandals of the "Arringatore" (page 46), of the Flamens at the Ara Pacis (page 52), and of the charioteer in the circus (page 47), had developed into more or less ordinary shoes (compare also the footwear of the hunter page 185).

Apart from sandals, both Greeks and Romans wore plain shoes made of soft leather, as is shown by the singer and his listeners on page 249, and by the actors of phlyacography on page 67. The lady's shoes depicted on the Hellenistic hydria on page 246 consist of a hard sole, a soft top and a tongue. The reveller on his way to the symposium wore larger boots which he then took off and placed under the kline (page 252), – no one would have dared to lie on the dining couch with his shoes on. They are soft boots without a sole and with high, turned down legs. Boots reaching up to the calf were not unknown: the revellers have put them on again for their return from the symposium (page 266), the archer wears them with several flaps hanging down (page 129), as does the beautiful Leagros on his horse (page 242, compare the ornamented riding boots of the Amazons page 133. The riding boy page 176 is barefoot, but his spurs are fastened to his ankles with straps).

The Romans took over the footwear from the Greeks and enriched and developed it according to the requirements of the people, the army and also of festive occasions (pages 52, 121, 196, 235).

233. Below: A young girl is tying her girdle and holding the pouched material, which is to fall over it, with her teeth.

235. Roman married couple, as on page 299. The woman wears an undergarment and a large cloak, which is like the Hellenistic cloak worn by the girl on page 234, even though it is greatly enriched by crossed-over pleats.

241. Compare the closely fitting fur coat worn by the herdsman on the right with the oblique fur coat of the herdsman above and also with the fur coat worn by the Teuton on page 148. Animal skins were worn by Dionysus and the Maenads in his retinue (pages 14, 242) – Heracles wore a lion's skin (page 138).

247. Tattoos – zigzag lines on the arms, small animals on the shoulders, rosettes on the knee – were handed down by the women of Thrace. They were also blonde, which the painter has here indicated with yellow paint. The woman comes from a picture showing Orpheus being killed by the women of Thrace.

MUSIC AND DANCE

Pages 248–260

Our word "music" comes from the Greek. Its connection with the Muses is significant, for the nine Muses were the inspiration, and also the protectresses, of all musical creation, including poetry, music itself, the dance and even scientific activities. They were venerated everywhere as the "Muses on the Helicon." The girl playing the lyre on the lekythos (page 250) is sitting on a rock and is therefore clearly marked as a muse from the Helicon (the name Terpsichore is also added in writing to the harp player underneath). Young people learned to make music at an early age – they learned to play instruments and to sing to their own accompaniment (pages 153, 248). Linus of Thebes was the mythical prototype of all music teachers, even if they did not all share his fate: he was killed for rebuking Heracles who unceremoniously hit him over the head with the instrument he was teaching him to play. Singing and playing nearly always went together; the cithara player sang and accompanied himself on the string instrument (page 249), and the poets were also called singers, and were indeed singers as the picture of Sappho and Alcaeus shows (page 105).

Neither music nor musical instruments was invented by the Greeks, for string and wind instruments were previously known to the Cretans and Oriental nations. The method of arranging notes and scales in certain ways was also taken over from the Orient. That the Greeks were aware of this is shown by the mention of Lydian and Phrygian melodies as opposed to Doric ones. Even the "blind singer" (like the singer from Chios, as he is called in the Homeric hymn) was known already in Egyptian culture as a musician type.

Three string instruments are most commonly depicted, especially in the representations of classical times: the lyre is a harp-like instrument with curved sides, which are connected by a fret from which the strings lead into a sound box (pages 105, 153, 248, 250, 251, 267). The ornamentation on this soundbox is reminiscent of the markings on a tortoise shell, from which Hermes created the first string instrument; with it he bewitched Apollo and then gave it to him, since when he is simply known as the God of the Cithara. The instrument was played by plucking the strings with a plectrum, the Greek plectron (pages 248, 249, 105, – a similar instrument to the one used today for the mandolin and zither), and fingering them with the other hand. The cithara has a large sound box, wide projecting side pieces and a large fret (page 249, compare page 266). The plectrum is here connected to the instrument by a long cord. The peg at the end of the fret served to tighten and tune the strings with the help of a tuning key (page 153). The harp of Terpsichore, with its triangular shape, curved hollow sound box, horizontal fret and diagonal strings of various lengths, is, on the one hand, reminiscent of a primeval instrument from the culture of the Cyclades, which dates back to 3000 B.C., and, on the other, of the almost unaltered but enlarged form of today's harp. It was played without a plectrum, the strings being plucked with both hands, as they are today.

The most common of the wind instruments was the flute (aulos) which the Romans also used and called tibia (page 54). The unusually long flute depicted with Euterpe, on the Roman Muses sarcophagus on page 255, is a kind of shawm which was used at the emperor's sacrifice (page 55). It is a double flute with two pipes of different lengths and was played through one mouthpiece by blowing through a wide band which was secured to the head by a cord (page 252). Boys learned to play the flute at an early age (page 153) and played the instruments at the men's symposium (page 252, 264). Men and hetaerai played the flute on their way home from the revels (pages 266, 267) and it was not scorned by the women and girls who played it in their chambers (page 227), or for the dance (page 253), although the blown-out cheeks distorted the face (compare the tuba player page 254), which is why Athena threw away the flutes. The double flute was kept in a special case consisting of three parts – two for the long pipes and one for the mouthpiece (pages 264, 278).

The Greek trumpet (salpinx) had a short mouthpiece, a long tube and a funnel-shaped opening (page 251). It was played on war-like occasions in ancient times the same way as it is today: by the trumpeter holding the instrument in his right hand and placing his left hand on his hip; the Greeks also blew with their heads high and slightly thrown back, exactly like the Roman trumpeter on page 254. The Etruscan relief on page 245 shows that the fife was also played.

The tympanum was used for the dance and was played by women (pages 257, 260) as well as men (page 66). It is a small hand drum, with hide stretched over a round frame exactly like today's tambourine. It was beaten with a flat hand. The crotalum (a kind of castanet) served as a percussion instrument and assisted the rhythmic movements of the dancers. It was mainly used by girls (page 257), but the man dancing at the symposium on page 266 holds it in his hands. Greek dancing was mainly connected with the practice of religious rites. There were solo dances, or round dances, including wild or even obscene ones, there were dances with several participants or with only two, but dances in which men and women participated together were almost, though not completely, unknown. The representations of the dancing Maenads, followers of Dionysus, outbid each other in the reproduction of ecstasy and passion. Pictures of this kind were also very popular with the Romans (page 259). The best examples are given by the reliefs on works of the so-called neo-Attic school, which exported copies and transformations of classical works from Athens to Rome, during the time of the early emperors.

253. Work of the Dancer painter. The short garment of the dancer is like the one on the relief on page 258.

255. The girl in the center is presumably Euterpe, with Muses in comic and tragic masks on the right and left.

260. The picture is the continuation of the scene on page 14.

SYMPOSIUM

Pages 261–267

The Greek symposium like the Roman convivium was a very characteristic form of male companionship. It fulfilled a definite function in the life of the individual and of the whole state. To know more of what went on above all Plato's "Symposium" should be read and compared with Xenophon's. It will then be realized how little it has to do with a student's club, to which it has been compared, even if it was exclusively made up of men and boys (except for the hetaerai who were included as dancers, musicians and acrobats, page 183), who drank heartily, sang songs (skolies) and elected a leader of the meeting – the symposiarch.

The invited guests gathered at the house of the host where they were joined by chance arrivals. They took off their shoes, reclined on the klines which were arranged in a horseshoe (see No. 214) and first of all enjoyed a sumptuous meal. Boy servants poured the wine from a large vessel in which the wine was mixed with water (mixing vessel – krater), for pure wine was not drunk. Each person had a cup or goblet, but the cups were also passed from one to the other on the right. The high points of the feast were the speeches, the subjects of which were chosen and allotted by the symposiarch who enforced suitably good order. The speakers improvised, probably often helped by the wine. Then came the dancers, exhibiting their skills and their charms, and when the effects of the wine were beginning to be felt they provided an amorous diversion, which apparently gave offense to no one. The feast lasted far into the night and afterwards the hetaerai, with music and torches, guided the dancing, singing revellers in "comos" to their homes.

261.   This picture is like the work of the Panaitios painter. The three black vessels on the lower edge of the picture are represented as though standing on a small dining table. The kantharos with two long ribbon handles is like the one carried by Dionysus (page 14, 233) or used by the priest for the offering (page 44). This one will also have served for the offering of pure wine to the gods, as will the two scyphi (compare the scyphus on page 181 and the vessel on the table at the symposium on page 264 above). The revellers drank from cups with contrasting rims and threw the dregs at the kottaboss utensils (see page 263 and no. 183).

262.   No symposium is here represented, but Achilles, robbed of his friend Patroclus, dining alone. There is a richly painted cone. The boards at the head and foot are like the ones on the kline of the Etruscan couple on page 289. On the "wall" are an Attic helmet, a shield with Gorgons, a sword in its scabbard and two small cloaks.

263.   Below: about the kottaboss game see page 183.

264.   This interior picture also belongs to the detailed representation of a symposium depicted on the outside of the bowl. The boy holds a double flute in his left hand, the position of his right is reminiscent of the dancing gesture in "comos" of the boy on page 265 below.
Below: The basin into which the toper is vomiting is on a stand. It is a large bowl with two handles and three legs (probably bronze), like the one used by the young doctor on page 286. (Compare with the washbowl on page 245 and with the cobbler's bowl on page 192, which stand on broad legs. They are probably made of clay).

265.   A ladle, similar to that of the cup bearer (see page 263) is being used. He holds a scyphus as a drinking cup in his hand (see page 261).

266.   The dancers are garlanded with twigs; they are returning home from the symposium, happily singing and dancing. The painter has inscribed their names.

267.   This is a particularly beautiful, classical picture. The torch carried by the boy on the right indicates that it is night. The plectrum (see page 248) of the lyre player can be clearly distinguished.

THE DIFFERENT AGES OF MAN

Pages 268–284

The representations of the different ages of man – youth, manhood and old age – show the approach and attitude towards the phenomena of age – realities as seen through the eye of the artist. These pictures, therefore, are works of art from different epochs and of different qualities, but, nevertheless, they are works of art. Everywhere there have always been children and old men, young women and old –

but have they always been represented in their true outward form? Have children always been shown as children, old men as old men and old women as old women? The problem – the different ages of man in ancient art – immediately becomes clear if we compare the two pictures of Hector taking leave of his parents (the picture by Euthymides page 122 and the picture by the Hector painter page 280) with Trojan reality. On both pictures Priam is depicted as an old man with thinning hair and a sparse beard (indicated by punctuation) and wearing a thick coat and warm shoes – on the later picture he is even shown with white hair. These outer attributes can be immediately recognized as the appearance of old age. And Hecuba? Even if she was considerably younger than her husband, she would still have been a mature woman when her grown-up son left for the war – but she is represented as a young woman without the slightest signs of age, and is recognizable as Hecuba only from the inscriptions. As late as 450 B.C. therefore, the artist did not dare, in spite of all biological proof, to represent the outer signs of an aging woman. The same applies to grandmother Ampharete (page 269): not one sign of old age can be seen, for the fine creases on the neck were not a sign of old age but of feminine charm and are also hardly ever absent from the portraits showing the immaculate beauty of the Goddess of Love. Some of the tombstones of the 5th and 4th centuries B.C. are enveloped in a mist of eternal youth (e.g., pages 274, 289) – it is impossible to ascertain the ages of the deceased, for it was not part of the intention of the artist to give any indication of it on the portraits. Men, on the other hand, if they died old, were, during this time, more and more often depicted with shaggy hair, lines on the forehead (page 281) and even with withered skin. This was the beginning of a new development which reached its zenith in Hellenistic times with the completely unclassical analysis of sculpture through the appearance in the face of every possible sign of old age (page 284 above). Not until this epoch (3rd, 2nd and 1st century B.C.) were the signs of age in women passionately sought, also, of course, in connection with the new trend of representing the lower social classes: poor market women, or the equally degenerate old woman ruined by drink (pages 282, 284). It is amazing how sculptured effects like the folds of a garment over hanging breasts, or emaciated skin, are here intensified to become deeply affecting. Pitiful ugliness became an instrument of virtuosity.

Numerous child portraits from the same epoch do not rely on the smallness of the child for characterization, but also represent individual traits (pages 270–271). This trend already became evident in the 4th century B.C. (page 269). Perhaps the small child on the lap of Ampharete could be included because of its almost embryonic head (about 400 B.C.), but most of the older pictures, almost without exception, represented children simply as small human beings (page 268 above). A type that dominates the whole of the ancient world emerges from the beginnings of Greek large-scale sculpture which heralded its advent with enormous figures in the second half of the 7th century B.C.: it is the kouros, the standing naked boy, the ephebe (page 295 right). The youthful male body kindled and inspired the development of Greek sculpture – a fact of more than artistic significance. The formulations evolved for the figure of the kouros prove their validity for other works not representing boys but older men, like the man carrying a calf on page 205: he is characterized as a man far beyond the age of an ephebe by his beard and coat, but not by his body. Even statues of women dating from this time give more the impression, apart from the clothes and their relationship to the body, of youthful male figures with appended breasts (page 233, 245).

In the archaic epoch the male image handed down from time immemorial was dominant; the classical added to the completion of the human "kosmos" by representing the female form. The child became included in the subclassical times of the 4th century B.C., and Hellenism developed the representation of the different ages of man, including senility.

The changes in Roman art cannot be as simply defined: the representation of individual facial peculiarities including the specific signs of old age was greatly encouraged by the inherited necessity of having ancestral portraits in the home (see page 212). Roman artists, also, of course, influenced by the Hellenistic age, therefore never hesitated to represent older women as older women, although they still used a little more restraint than in their portraits of men, which always reflected the appropriate signs of age as well as revealing private characteristics (see page 123), especially in the not classically determined epochs. On the other hand, it is not easy to realize that the Emperor Augustus was about 50 years old at the time the statue at the Primaporta was created, and the enchanting portrait of the youth on page 117 can hardly be inferior in form to a Greek youth portrait. There were, therefore, also Roman trends, especially under the emperors, to emphasize the youthful in the classical manner.

268 and following. Also compare the child portraits with the pictures showing the treatment of children, pages 224–225.

270. Compare the game with the goose, page 225.

272. Front view of the pleasant face of the girl from Antium on page 275.
Below: A victorious youth taking the wreath from his head. The right hand can still be seen above left. The circular holes served to secure the victor's wreath and the separately prepared hair.

274. The lekythos (pages 5, 170, 229, 301) is a small vessel which was used in the cult of the dead. Seen here is a monumental marble copy used as a gravestone.

275. Head of the figure seen from the front on page 272 above.

277. The boy is holding a strigilis (see pages 131, 189, 230) in his left hand, and an aryballos (see pages 189, 230) on a string in his right.

278. White lekythoi are Attic vessels with colored decorations on a white chalk background. The products of the lekythoi workshops belong to the most beautiful of the 5th century B.C. Other paintings of this kind on page 250 above, pages 268–302 above.

280. Hector's farewell, compare also the picture by Euthymides on page 122. Hector is holding a stemless drinking bowl in his hand, like the one on page 252.

DISEASES, DEATH AND TOMBS

Pages 285–304

It is amazing how similar, and, in many cases, even how alike, ancient surgical instruments are to the ones in use today. This implies that the simple use of these instruments was already discovered thousands of years ago, but it also means that the direct and live connection between modern and ancient medicine is, to a certain extent, figuratively speaking, presented before us. This is not only a question of inherited medical terms, which are constantly being reformed and are unintelligible to those without a knowledge of Greek, but of deeper connections, of scientific knowledge discovered long ago and still valid to this day. The "Oath of Hippocrates" sworn by the ancient doctors defines the tasks and duties of medicine in classical form almost exactly as they are defined today – apart from the invocation of Apollo and his son Asclepius.

Asclepius (Aesculapius) is a god and a doctor. His servants are priests and doctors at the same time. The sanctuaries of Asclepius (Asclepiaeum) are places of worship and also of healing, for their furnishings relate to the cult as well as to the treatment of physical and spiritual ailments. Lying-in rooms for treatments, arrangements for the so-called "temple sleep," were found in Epidaurus, the most famous of the healing places of the 4th century B.C., in Cos where Hippocrates (460–327 B.C.) lived and taught, and in Pergamum, where Galenus, the physician of Marcus Aurelius and Commodus, came from.

The close connection between healing and worship, so that the god was considered to effect the cure, was never rejected, but neither did it ever, and especially after the end of the 5th century B.C., prevent the "priests" from recognizing, exploring and sometimes solving, the problems of medicine. Thus they soon put medicine on a scientific foundation, and it is this foundation that has retained its validity beyond the times of the Greeks and the Romans, into the middle ages and up to the present day. Even Arabic culture gained from Greek knowledge. Some of the books by Galenus are only preserved in an Arabic translation.

123.   Achilles, himself, tends the wound of his friend Patroclus (page XXXII).

227.   Greek doctor of Roman times in front of his medicine and instrument cupboard (page XLVII).

285.   The representation of the hunch-backed beggar, a wretched pitiful creature, belongs to a time which, on the one hand, did not hesitate to reproduce also the ugly manifestations of human life and, on the other, turned for artistic inspiration towards the lower and lowest social stratum.
Below: This relief is consecrated to Asclepius. It shows wailing women on the left, the sick woman lying on a bed in the center, and beside her Asclepius, himself, making healing gestures – he is the largest figure. Behind him is his daughter Hygeia, the Goddess of Health.

286.   A clinic in the proper sense of the word: A misshapen dwarf comes to see the doctor about his troubles. He carries a hare on his shoulder – the fee was paid in kind instead of money.
Below: A young assistant is cutting a man's arm with a sharp knife. A large bowl stands underneath to catch the blood.

The deceased was entitled to claim a dignified funeral from the living: this consisted of the relatives gathering in the house (page 288), the lying in state (prothesis, expositio, pages 288 below, 289) and the lamentation itself (conclamatio) followed by the ekphora (the conducting of the body to the cemetery) and finally the burial. The fantasy of the painters was, from early times on, inspired by these significant ceremonies rooted in the imaginative world of religion. The first "contents" in the drawings dating back to the time of geometric art (8th century B.C.) are representations of burial ceremonies depicted on vessels which were themselves used in the cult of the dead as grave-stones, for the offering of wine at the grave or as a gift to the dead. The body, or the ashes if it was burned, was placed in a coffin (page 289). Sarcophagus art – the art of developing the orna-mentation of the simple coffin into specific art forms – flourished at all times; it was developed by the Romans into a minor industry, and was also, later, taken over by the Christians (e.g., pages 112, 186, 223, 225, 225).

The grave itself and a memorial were part of the claim to which the dead were entitled. The Greeks, as well as the Romans, felt the need to bury their dead, whenever possible, in the same environment in which they had lived – in the family circle. The large necropolis known to us, the cemetery on the Eridanus in Athens and the great road of graves in the south of Rome – the Via Appia, to name only two out of many, therefore mainly contain large vaults in which the members of a whole family or of a tribe are buried. It is also usual to find a common grave for soldiers fallen in battle: the responsibility of the living to the dead was here taken over and fulfilled by the state. The simple grave mound on the edge of the plain of Marathon (page 290) is as much an example of this as the mighty lion of Chaeronea (page 291). The emperor Augustus had a large mausoleum built for himself and his family during his lifetime in the very distinctive form of a circular building (also used by the emperor Hadrian about 150 years later in the Castle of St. Angelo), whereby he followed an old tradition going back far beyond the Etruscans into time immemorial. If religion is the taskmaster of art, then the demands of the cult of the dead contributed in no small way, producing a style of art which constantly presented new forms, chiefly concerned with funeral figures and reliefs. Many of the earlier figures of boys and youths from archaic times (7th and 6th century B.C.) previously falsely described as "Apollines" (page 295), of which a large number have been preserved, are funeral figures representing the deceased as a young man. If all the statues of ancient times, including those of deities, victors and other honored personages, were classified according to their purposes, funeral figures would constitute one third of the whole number. The custom of placing statues on graves was taken over by the Romans from the Greeks (pages 46, see No. 299). These figures stood on stone pedestals from which the reliefs of the Themistoclean wall on pages 157, 179 originate.

Reliefs representing the deceased, by himself or in a group with the living, were used as tomb memorials by the Greeks and Romans in all times, even if the custom was here and there temporarily interrupted by laws forbidding this luxury, as for instance in Athens at the end of the 4th century B.C. Greek tomb reliefs: pages 126, 276, 277, 47, 269, 298; Roman tomb reliefs: pages 194 to 197, 227, 235, 299, 300; the relief on page 96 also stems from a grave.

287. A procession of men with right arms raised in accompaniment to songs (the mouths of the men are open).

288. Three women are standing and sitting on each side of the veiled woman in the center; she is the chief mourner, the mother of the deceased. A woman with a small child on her arm stands behind her.
Below: Broken narrow pinax showing a tree with sacred sashes on the right.

289. Here the coffin is in the shape of a kline, and the group of figures on the top is the removable lid.

290. The picture shows the original grave mound. The steps were added at a later time to facilitate the mounting of the hill. These steps are definitely not original for grave mounds were not raised to be climbed.
Below: Cleobulus was the "tyrant" of Lindus, one of the "Seven Wise Men." He lived about 600 B.C. The tomb was built later. The diameter is about 30 yards.

291.   In the Aedicula the relief originally in front of the high pillar with a bull on top, as a memorial, is now missing.

293.   Young Marcellus, who was the nephew of the Emperor and had been chosen to succeed him, was the first to be entombed in the Augustus mausoleum.

294.   The sepulcher of the Julii consists of a solid pedestal with reliefs on all four sides, on top of this ia a kind of tetrapylon (a structure of four gateways) with a monopteros (circular structure with simple column arrangement without cella).
Below: Eurysaces was a baker who supplied the state; representations of measuring vessels form the base for the superstructure shaped like a baking oven of this scurrilous sepulcher.

295.   Below: The boy wears a short chiton with a single girdle, as worn by the working part of the population. His features are not Greek (compare with the boy rider on page 176), therefore a slave is probably represented who once stood beside his master, of whom nothing now remains.

296.   The lion of Miletus is one of the most beautiful representations of animals from ancient times. Below: servant girls in the appropriate costume of the time (see page 298).

297.   Girl with a round box (the lid is on the floor below), probably scattering incense, as on page 50.

298.   The lightly veiled woman is Hegeso, the deceased; she is taking an object out of a small rectangular casket with a hinged lid. The object is not part of the sculpture but was merely painted on: probably a piece of jewelry, a necklace or some such thing, that gave her pleasure in life.

299.   The relief figures seen from the front are repetitions of three-dimensional funeral figures, as they were often to be found in cemeteries.

301.   The picture shows a tomb stele with a palmette head in the style of the "stele Giustiniani" on page 297, which also stood on a step foundation. The deceased herself sits on the steps in silent grief.

302.   The woman on the left carries an alabastron and a so-called smegmatotheke as well as an ointment container.

303.   Orestes, in the presence of his sister Electra and his friend Pylades, who is sitting on the steps of the tomb, swears, with raised sword, to avenge his father's murder.

INDEX

The numbers given refer to pages and to the numbered references in the text.

PLATES

Zeus abducting the boy Ganymede. Painted terra cotta group from Olympia (Museum), c. 470 B.C.

Zeus. Head of the bronze statue found on Cape Artemesium, Athens, National Museum, c. 460 B.C.

Hera. Large head from the votive group in the Heraion at Olympia, after 600 B.C.

Apollo assisting in battle. Central figure on the West Pediment of the Temple of Zeus, Olympia (Museum), c. 460 B.C.

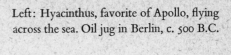

Left: Hyacinthus, favorite of Apollo, flying across the sea. Oil jug in Berlin, c. 500 B.C.

Right: Artemis, "Diana of Ostia". Marble statue in Rome, Museo Nazionale delle Terme, from the time of Hadrian.

Artemis hunting a deer. Attic votive relief in Kassel, c. 400 B.C.

Athena standing in front of boundary stone. Marble votive relief from the Acropolis in Athens, c. 460 B.C.

Athena assisting Theseus. Cup of
Aison in Madrid, c. 400 B.C.

Nike, goddess of victory, with armor. Small wine jug
in Copenhagen, early 5th century B.C.

Nike, marble acroterium from the Hall of Zeus
in the Agora, Athens, Athens Agora Museum,
c. 390 B.C.

Nike drifting down from pillar. Work of Paionios,
in Olympia, c. 420 B.C.

Hermes with the newly born Dionysus. Original work of Praxiteles in Olympia, c. 340 B.C.

Hermes Logios, the God as orator. Head of "Hermes Ludovisi" in Rome, Mus. Naz. Roman copy of an Attic original, c. 450 B.C.

Demeter and Core at the sending forth of Triptolemus. Large Eleusinian votive relief, Athens, Nat. Mus., c. 440 B.C.

Triptolemus in the winged snake chariot. Dish in the Vatican, c. 430 B.C.

Dionysus leading Hephaestus back to the Olympus. Jug in Munich, c. 440–430 B.C.

Maenad performing an ecstatic dance. From an amphora in Munich, c. 500 B.C.

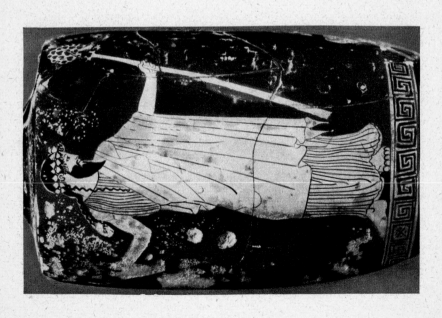

Dionysus. Lekythos by Hermonax in Palermo, about 480–470 B.C.

Aphrodite rising from the sea. Relief on the front of the "Ludovisi Throne" in Rome, Mus. Naz., c. 470–460 B. C.

Aphrodite bathing.

Right: Goddess disrobing, terra cotta figure in Berlin, c. 150 B.C.

Below: Goddess crouching, after an original of Doidalsas of Bithynia, in Rome, Mus. Naz., c. 260 B.C.

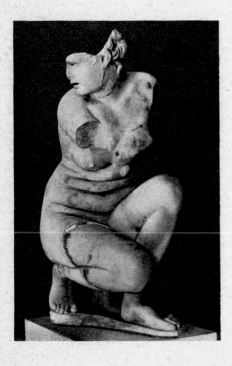

Ares and Aphrodite (Mars and Venus) in tender embrace. Pompeian mural, 1st century A. D.

Above: Erotes. Below: Pluto and Persephone. Amphora in Paris, after 500 B.C.

Nyx, goddess of the night in a battle with giants. Section of the north frieze of the great altar of Pergamum in Berlin, c. 200 B.C.

Poseidon, lord of the seas. Hellenistic marble statue from the isle of Melos in Athens, Nat. Mus., 2nd century B.C.

Above: The three-bodied sea monster from one of the pediments of the Acropolis at Athens, c. 575 B.C.

Left: Pan, the god of pastures in the form of a ram. Terra cotta statue from Eretria in Berlin, c. 300 B. C.

Selene, goddess of the moon, driving across the sea. Mixing urn in Athens, Nat. Mus., second half of 5th century.

Sol, the Roman sun-god rising from the sea in his horse-drawn chariot. Relief from a coat of arms on a statue in Rome.

Mithras killing the bull. Marble group from a Mithraic sanctuary in Ostia (Museum), time of Hadrian.

The Acropolis at Athens, the temple of Athena Parthenos from the southeast, in the center the Olympieum.

The Parthenon on the Acropolis at Athens. West front seen from northwest, c. 450–440 B.C.

Above: The Propylaea of the Acropolis. Central building from the west, c. 430 B.C. Below: Propylaea of Eleusis, erected by Emperor Marcus Aurelius, c. 175 A.D.

Above: The Hieron at Olympia from the southeast, early Greek. Below: Inside the Temple of Zeus at Olympia, c. 460 B.C.

Above: The Erechtheum on the Acropolis, Athens, from the southwest, late classical. Below: The Hieron from Delos, above the Temple of Apollo.

Right: North Portico of the Erechtheum. Portico for side entrance from the east.

Below: The Temple of Nike in front of the Propylaea of the Acropolis, late classical.

Treasury of the Athenians in Delphi; left: the entrance. Right: View from the interior onto the Phaedriades, c. 490 B.C.

Castalia, sacred fountain near the Temple of Apollo at Delphi.

Kallichoros, sacred well beside the Propylaea at Eleusis.

33

Above left: Tholos (circular building) in Delphi, c. 400 B.C. Above right: Steps hewn out of rock at Eleusis.

Left: Telesterion (Temple of the Mysteries) at Eleusis, step-seats in the interior.

In the sacred grove, Olympia. Above: Philippeion, erected after 338 B.C. Below: Entrance to stadium.

The Grotto of the Nymphs at Vari, an underground and sacred rock grotto dedicated to Pan, Appollo and the nymphs.

Within the sanctuary of Apollo at Delos. Above: The Lion Terrace, marble work dating from the 7th century B.C. Below: Exedra. Seat for resting, Hellenistic period.

A memorial on the sacred path in Delphi erected to commemorate the victory gained over the Persians at Plataea.

Above: The Capitol of Ostia in the Forum of the city, time of Hadrian. Below: Sacred precincts, altar and temple of Vespasian in Pompeii, 1st century A.D.

Temple of Jupiter Heliopolitanus (Baal) at Baalbeck (Lebanon) 2nd century A.D. Above: View of the Great Court. Below: Niches and colonnades surrounding the Great Court.

Syrian-Roman temple buildings in the Lebanon (Hoessn Sfiri). Above: Front of temple. Below: Interior, adytum with staircase and side entrance to crypt. 2nd century A.D.

Vaulted sanctuary, nave and apse of the Basilica at the Porta Maggiore in Rome.
1st century A.D.

Above: Family visiting sanctuary in the country. Votive relief in Munich, about 200 B.C.
Below: Dedication of a tripod for equestrian victory. Relief in Athens Nat. Mus., about 350 B.C.

Orestes begging for shelter in Delphi. Water jug in Berlin, 4th century B.C.

Priest at sacrificial altar. Picture on a dish in Palermo, about 500 B.C.

Man praying, from Arcadia. Bronze statuette in Berlin, c. 500 B.C.

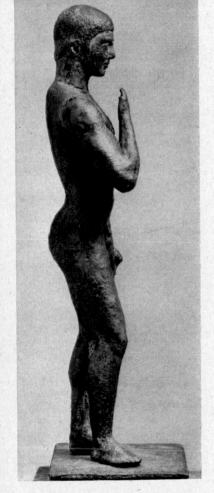

Man praying. Statuette in New York. Early classical, c. 470 B.C.

Man praying, dressed in tunic and toga. Bronze statue of Avles Metels in Florence, 1st century B.C.

Greek Priestess. The tombstone of Polyxena from Boeotia, beginning of 4th century B.C.

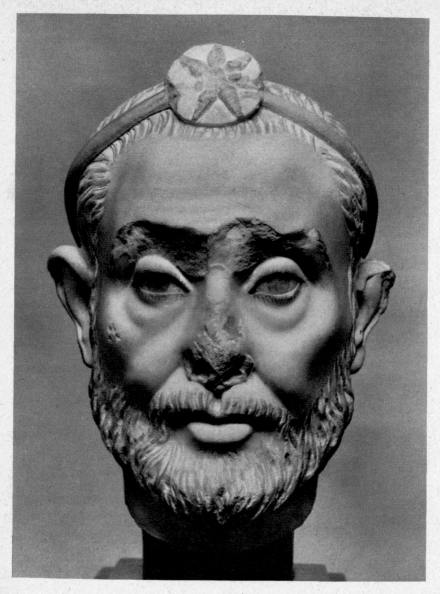

Portrait of a priest. Marble head from Alexandria in Berlin, 3rd century A.D.

Virgo Vestalis Maxima, Chief of the Vestal Virgins, in Rome Mus. Naz., c. 200 A.D.

Young woman with incense burner. Side of the so-called Ludovisi Throne in Rome, Mus. Naz., c. 470–460 B.C.

Priestesses in front of altar. Late Antique ivory reliefs on a Consular Diptych.

Procession of priests, sacrificial servant and Pontifex Maximus. Relief from the Altar of Peace of Emperor Augustus at Rome, 13–9 B.C.

Procession of the Imperial Retinue. Relief from the Altar of Peace of Emperor Augustus (Ara Pacis Augustae) at Rome, 13–9 B.C.

Above: A general offering a sacrifice at the Altar of Mars. Relief in Paris, 1st century B.C.
Below: Suovetaurilia. Relief from the time of Claudius in Paris, 1st century B.C.

The Emperor offering a sacrifice on the Capitol in Rome. Roman relief from a Triumphal Arch of Marcus Aurelius, Palace of the Conservators, 178 A.D.

Roman boy assisting at sacrifice (Camillus) with wine jug and sacrificial dish. Pompeian mural, 1st century A.D.

The Greek Theater of Epidaurus, 4th century B.C. Above: Scene and auditorium. Below: View from top tier onto the auditorium, orchestra and stage.

The Theater of Dionysus, Athens. Above: Aerial view. Below: Marble thrones assigned to the priests (Proedria).

Roman theater. Above: In Orange. View of stage buildings. Below: In Vaison la Romaine, colonnade.

Small theater at Pompeii, entrance for the Chorus, staircase leading to auditorium.

Roman Amphitheater at Arles. Above: Tiered seats and ambulatory. Below: Aerial view of interior and exterior.

Amphitheater. Above: Nîmes, outer wall with main entrance, 1st century A.D. Below: Colosseum, Amphitheater of Flavian in Rome, 1st century A.D.

The "Arena", Amphitheater in Verona, outer and inner walls, 3rd century A.D.

Performances. Above: Scene from a tragedy. Fragment of a vase in Dresden. Below: Scene from a comedy. Amphora in Berlin, c. 500 B.C.

Above: Phlyacography, burlesque enacted on a raised stage. Mixing bowl from Southern Italy, in Berlin. Below: Portrait of a famous actor. Relief, time of the Emperors, in Dresden.

Man playing tambourine. Part of a musical scene by Dioscurides of Samos, Mosaic in Naples.

Masked actor, Southern Italian Phlyacography. Mixing bowl in Vienna.

Terra cotta copy of a comedy mask
from Priene in Berlin.

Greek comedy actor with mask.
Terra cotta figure in Adolphseck.

Marching warrior as a figure of Greek comedy. Hellenistic terra cotta statuette from Asia Minor in Berlin.

Animal baiting in the amphitheater. Left: Baiting of lions; right: Baiting of deer. Late antique Consular diptych in Leningrad and London.

Emperor presiding at games. Left: at a chariot race; right: at a fight between bears and men.
Late antique Consular diptych.

Chariot race in a circus, dense crowds near the turning point. Roman relief from the time of the Emperors in Foligno.

Above: Trained monkey driving chariot pulled by camels. Relief in Rome. Below: Four competing charioteers. Mosaic in Rome, 2nd century A.D.

Charioteer of quadriga in circus just before the turning point (metae) wearing helmet and breast plate. Section of a relief on a tomb in the Lateran, end of 1st century A.D.

Doric Order. Above: The Temple of Hephaestus in Athens, complete view from southwest. Below: Colonnade, Temple of Poseidon at Sunium, both c. 430 B.C.

Doric Order. Details from the Parthenon; above: frieze; below: stylobate.

Doric Order. Southwest corner of the Parthenon; left: the west pediment; right: the south elevation, first metope depicting the battle with centaurs 450–440 B.C.

Above: Doric triglyphs on the Temple of Hephaestus, c. 430 B.C. Below: Anta of the Propylaea on the Acropolis, c. 430 B.C.

Doric capital. Exterior colonnade of the Propylaea on the Acropolis, Athens.

Ionic capital. Inner colonnade of the Propylaea on the Acropolis, Athens, c. 430 B.C.

Ionic Order. Above: Anta from Miletus in Berlin, 6th century B.C. Below: Base of column from the northern colonnade of the Erechtheum in Athens.

Propylaeum leading to the Athena Sanctuary of Pergamum. Reconstruction in Berlin. Below: Doric order; above: Ionic order, c. 200 B.C.

Above: The Caryatid's porch of the Erechtheum. Below: Corinthian order – Olympieum, Athens, Graeco-Roman.

Above: Example of capital (Corinthian) from the Tholos of Epidaurus, 4th century B.C. Below: The Tower of the Winds at Athens, exterior; marble vaulting of the interior.

Rainwater spouts. Above: Head of ram on the older Telesterium of Eleusis, 6th century B.C. Below: Head of a lion from the cornice of the Temple of Zeus, Olympia.

Above: Upper acroterion of a temple. Terracotta group in Berlin, c. 500 B.C. Below: Antefixae from the Temple of Apollo at Veii. Rome, Villa Giulia, c. 500 B.C.

Wall buildings. Above: Cyclopean wall of the citadel of Tiryns, 14th–13th century B.C. Below: City wall with watch towers of Eleutherae facing the fields, 4th century B.C.

Above: Cistern by the theatre of Delos. Below: Wall of the library of Athens with shelf recesses. Time of Hadrian.

Roman Temples. Above: Round temple by the Tiber in Rome. Below: Temple built on a podium with staircase leading up to it, "Maison Carrée" in Nîmes, 1st century A.D.

Temple of Saturn, front elevation with six Ionic columns on a high podium, in front the rostra. Forum in Rome.

Triumphal Arches. Above: Orange, 1st century A.D. Below: Triumphal Arch of Constantine in Rome, 4th century A.D.

Above: Porta Nigra, Northern gateway of the Trèves city wall, 313–316 A.D. Below: Market gate from Miletus. Reconstruction in Berlin, c. 165 A.D.

Viaduct, "Pont du Gard" at Nîmes, 1st century A.D.

Sacred well of the Nymphs in Nîmes.

Peirene, large well building from Corinth, late antique style.

Representation of the Colosseum, a Roman relief from the tomb of the Haterii. Rome, the Lateran, 1st century A.D.

Above: Wreath with fruit on entablature from the Pirene in Corinth. Below: Roman composite capital in the thermae of Caracalla, probably 3rd century A.D.

City streets. Above: Stabian street in Pompeii. Below: Street of wells in Ostia.

Streets in Ostia. Above: Street of the house of Diana (Town center). Below: Street of the Balconies: large dwelling house on the corner.

Warehouses in Ostia. Above: Street front of a large warehouse. Below: Oil store with sunken terra cotta storage vessels.

Taverns in Ostia. Above: Inn near the Forum. Below: Thermopolium in the Diana street, 3rd century A.D.

Above: Fishmonger's shop in Ostia. Below: Hall and courtyard of a club house (Scuola del Trajano) in Ostia.

Public Buildings. Above: Stabian Thermae in Pompeii. Below: Public convenience in the Forum Thermae in Ostia, 2nd century A.D.

Homer. Marble head in Munich, from a votive present of Mikythos of Rhegium, c. 460 B.C.

Alcaeus and Sappho with instruments. Wine vessel in Munich. From the school of Brygos, after 480 B.C.

Aesop, the fabulist, in conversation
with a fox. Dish in the Vatican,
c. 470 B.C.

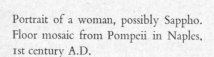

Portrait of a woman, possibly Sappho.
Floor mosaic from Pompeii in Naples,
1st century A.D.

Sophocles, the dramatist (d. 406 B.C.). Statue in the Lateran. Roman copy of the statue which was erected in 330 at the theater of Athens.

Greek philosopher. Head from a bronze statue, 3rd century B.C., in Athens, Nat. Mus.

Euripides, the dramatist (d. 406 B.C.). Marble head in Rome, Mus. Naz., 4th century B.C.

Above: Socrates at Diotima's. Bronze ornament on a wooden chest in Naples.
Below: Phidias (?), Head of a Centaur with the characteristics of a portrait. From one of the metopes on the Parthenon, c. 440 B.C.

Left: Philosopher in Delphi. Hellenistic terra cotta statuette in Berlin.

Right: Unknown Greek philosopher, Hellenistic.

Demosthenes, the Attic orator (d. 322 B.C.). Marble copy of the Bronze Statue by Polyeuktos erected in Athens 280 B.C.

Above: Roman scholar with scrolls. Relief on a sarcophagus, 3rd century A.D. Below: Meeting of scholars. Roman mosaic in Rome, Villa Albani.

Hellenic ruler. Head of a bronze statue from Delos in Athens, Nat. Mus., 1st cent. B.C.

Head of man wearing laurel wreath (priest?) Athens, Nat. Mus. Original Hellenistic marble sculpture.

Hellenistic ruler in heroic stance. Bronze statue in Rome, Mus. Naz., Greek original c. 150 B.C.

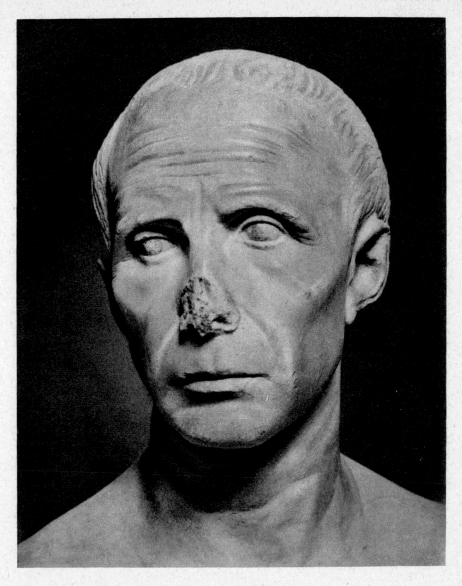

"Caesar of Accireale". Roman marble head from the time of the dictator, end of the 1st century B.C., possibly representing Caesar himself.

Augustus in armor, marble statue at Rome, Vatican, end of the 1st century B.C. Relief on the breastplate depicts the sun god driving his chariot beneath the god of the heavens.

Young Roman from the house of Augustus at the dedication of the Augustan peace altar. North side of the Ara Pacis Augustae. Reconstruction in Rome, 13–9 B.C.

Portraits of Roman emperors from the 1st century A.D.

Claudius (41–54 A.D.) as Jupiter wearing an oak wreath (Corona Civica). Head from the marble statue from the Civita Lavinia in Rome, Vatican.

Nero. (54–68 A.D.). Portrait head from the Palatine in Rome, Mus. Naz.

Portraits of Roman emperors of the
2nd century A.D.

Trajan (98–117). Marble head from Ostia,
sculpted soon after the emperor's death.

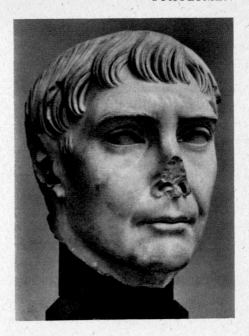

Hadrian (117–138). Marble head in Rome,
Mus. Naz.

Portraits of Roman emperors of the 2nd and 3rd centuries A.D.

Marcus Aurelius (161–180): Marble head from Hadrian's villa in Tivoli, Rome, Mus.Naz.

Gallienus (253–268). Marble head from the house of the Vestals by the Forum Romanum, Rome, Mus. Naz.

Two emperors embracing, possibly Diocletian (284–305) and Maximianus, co-regent since 285. Porphyry group in the Vatican, c. 300 A.D.

Above: fully armed warriors ready for combat playing a board-game, Ajax and Achilles. Amphora by Exekias in the Vatican, c. 540–530 B. C. Below: Fitting of breastplate. Hector between Priam and Hecuba. Amphora by Euthymides in Munich, c. 510 B.C.

Young man being presented with the arms of the Hoplites, Neoptolemos and Odysseus. Interior picture of a bowl by Duris, in Vienna, c. 480 B.C.

Attending to a wounded man, Achilles dressing the wounds of Patroclus. Interior picture of the Sosias bowl in Berlin, c. 510 B.C.

123

Tomb of a young warrior wearing Attic helmet.
Marble relief in Athens, Nat. Mus. c. 500 B.C.

Statue in honor of a warrior wearing
Corinthian helmet, Leonidas (?) Sparta,
Museum, c. 475 B.C.

Votive portrait of a warrior wearing bellshaped breastplate and Ionic helmet from Samos, Berlin, Altes Museum, c. 500 B.C.

Reverse of the portrait above.

Armed Spearman. Tombstone of the Athenian Aristion. Work by Aristocles. Athens, Nat. Mus., c. 500 B.C.

Young man carrying spear and wearing breastplate, Achilles. Picture on a vase by the Achilles Painter in the Vatican, c. 450–440 B.C.

The large circular shield of the Greek warriors.

Young attendant taking shield out of its protective covering. Early classical. Interior picture of a bowl at Bologna.

Circular shield on its stand in front of returning warrior. Attic jug (pelike) in San Francisco, early classical.

Young man putting on greaves.
Interior picture of the Oltos bowl
in Berlin, c. 520 B.C.

Young man dressed as an
archer stringing his bow.
Interior picture of Attic
bowl in London, before
500 B.C.

Amazon in Phrygian costume in a lunging position.
Attic jug (pelike) in Munich, c. 390 B.C.

Amazon drawing her bow in crouching stance.
Attic Amphora in Munich, c. 420 B.C.

Above: Horsemen carrying lances on the march. Attic Amphora in the Vatican, after 500 B.C.
Below: Young horseman carrying whip. Etruscan mural from Tarquinia (Tomba del Barone),
c. 500 B.C.

Left: Horseman with lance (Doryphoros) beside his horse. Votive relief from Argos in Athens, Nat. Mus., c. 400 B.C.

Rider calming a rearing horse. Relief from the West frieze of the Parthenon by Phidias.

A mounted fight with spears, Amazon thrusting short spear (Akontion). Late Attic Amphora in Rome, c. 400 B.C.

Above: Harnessing the chariot at the departure of the warrior. Attic water jug (Hydria) in Madrid c. 500 B.C. Below: Warrior, with shield on his back, in a chariot and Athena behind the horses. Attic jug in Copenhagen, after 500 B.C.

Armed man jumping off moving chariot in practice. Relief from the Parthenon frieze by Phidias.

Battle scene; kneeling warriors attacking, one man wounded.

Fully armed spearman attacking.
Bronze statue from Dodona in Berlin,
c. 500 B.C.

From the West Pediment of the Temple of Aphaia, Aegina, in Munich, c. 490 B.C.

Hoplites in battle (close combat).
Chalk relief in Dresden. 6th century B.C.

Battle scenes. Above: Sword used for cutting, Hercules fighting the Amazons. Attic Amphora at San Francisco, c. 510 B.C. Below: Attack and defense. Picture on a vase in Athens, c. 400 B.C.

Roman Parade helmet (bronze) from Heddernheim, in Frankfurt.

Roman Parade helmet, iron with bronze
ornamentation from Heddernheim, in Frankfurt, time of the Emperors.

Roman Legionaries on the march. Relief on the column of Marcus Aurelius, Rome, 176 A.D.

Roman Cavalry, some dismounted, fighting barbarians. Relief on the column of Marcus Aurelius, Rome, 176 A.D.

Above: The victory of a Roman general and his army over barbarians. "Battle sarcophagus of Ludovisi", Rome, Mus. Naz., c. 250 A.D.

Left: Roman army building a raft. Relief from the column of Trajan in Rome, 113 A.D.

Army gathered to listen to emperor's address (Adlocutio). Relief from the column of Trajan in Rome, 113 A.D.

Reliefs from the passage of the Arch of Titus in Rome. Above: Triumphal entry of the army into Rome with spoils from Jerusalem. Below: Titus riding in the triumphal procession in a quadriga, crowned by Victory and led by the Dea Roma.

Praetorian Guard surrounded by Roman genii. Relief from the Porta Triumphalis which was restored by Domitian (81–96 A.D.), Capitol Museum.

Above: Gallic chieftain in death agony. Head of the "dying Gaul", Rome, Mus. Cap. Pergamum sculpture, end of 3rd century B.C. Below: Head of a dying Persian. Original sculpture by the Pergamum school of art, c. 200 B.C. Rome, Mus. Naz.

Gallic chieftain killing his wife and himself. Marble group (Gallic Ludovisi) in Rome, Mus. Naz.
Copy of a work from Pergamum, 3rd century B.C.

Teuton prisoner, young lord in fur cloak. Roman relief on a monument commemorating a victory, Rome Vatican, early 2nd century A.D.

Ancient Teuton. Head of the relief on the front of the battle sarcophagus of Portonaccio in Rome, Mus. Naz., c. 175 A.D.

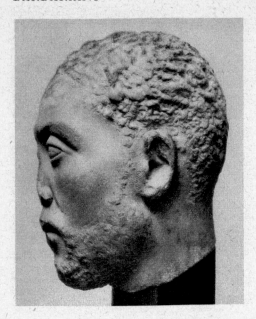

Memnon, a Negro from Ethiopia, pupil and friend of Herodes Atticus. Marble head from the Thyreatis (Peloponnesus) in Berlin, Greek work.

Old Negro, cameo (Karneol), 1st century B.C.

Old schoolmaster teaching with writing tablet and style. Bowl by the Panaitios painter in Berlin, c. 500 B.C.

Athena with style and folding tablet. Attic Amphora in Berlin, c. 480 B.C.

Instruction given by reading from a scroll to attentive pupils. Large cup with pictures by the Panaitios painter in Berlin, c. 490 B.C.

Solo lessons in playing the lyre, singing to the accompaniment as a flute, hearing a pupil reciting epic verse, young teacher making notes. Duris bowl in Berlin, c. 480 B.C.

Man beating boy with a sandal. Attic jug in Berlin, end of 6th century B.C.

Old Silenus beating young one with a strap. Part of a Roman sarcophagus relief in Rome, Museo Capitolino, 2nd century A.D.

The stadium at Delphi: original plan 4th century B.C., present plan 2nd century A.D. Above: Overall view of the oval (sphendone) towards the starting point. Below: Step-seats in the auditorium with view of oval.

Above: Court of the Palaestra at Olympia. Plan 4th century B.C. Below: Large basin for cold baths in the Delphi gymnasium. Plan 4th century B.C.

Representations of games. Reliefs from the base of a statue in Athens c. 510 B.C. Above: Ball game with two teams. Centre: Standing jump, wrestling, preliminary exercise for throwing the javelin. Below: Entertainment in the Palaestra: boys setting a dog against a cat.

Scenes from the Palaestra.

Boy with javelins, the act of releasing the javelin, boy with discus. Amphora by the Cleophrades painter in Munich, c. 500 B. C.

Classic javelin thrower, slinging the javelin. Interior picture of a bowl in Berlin, c. 430 B.C.

Scenes from the Palaestra.

Boy examining javelin before throwing it, boy about to throw discus, about to throw the javelin. Amphora by the Cleophrades painter in Munich, c. 500 B.C.

Below: Getting into position to throw discus. Attic Amphora, c. 500 B.C.

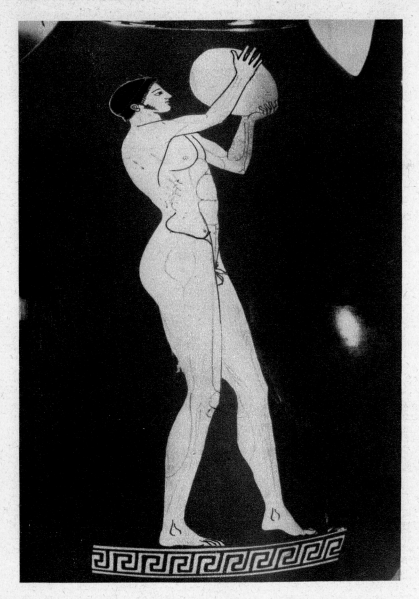

Gathering momentum to hurl the discus with both hands. Amphora by the "Berlin Painter" in the Vatican, c. 500 B.C.

Throwing the discus, shortly before releasing the disc. Etruscan bronze statuette in Adolphseck, c. 500 B. C.

Panathenaic prize amphora. Within view: end of boxing match with opponent knocked out. Attic, c. 530 B.C., in Berlin.

Above: Exchange of blows in boxing match. Panathenaic prize amphora in Berlin, c. 530 B.C.
Below: End of boxing match because of surrender of opponent. Attic bowl in New York,
c. 530 B.C.

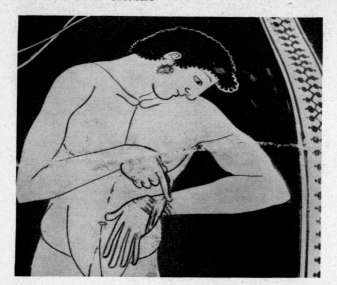

Left: Preparation for boxing match, putting on of fist straps. Amphora by the Cleophrades painter c. 500 B.C.

Punching chin with outstretched arm. From a picture representing a fight with centaurs, c. 460 B.C., in Florence, Mus. Archaeol.

Boxer resting, battered and exhausted from the fight. Bronze statue by Apollonius of Athens, end of the 1st century B.C.

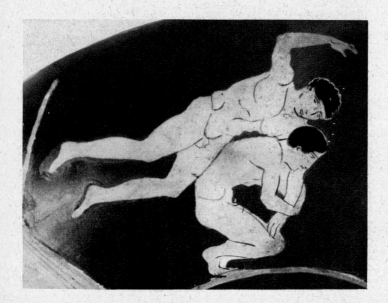

Scenes from the wrestling ring. Above: Opponents measuring up at the beginning of fight.
Bowl by the potter Nikosthenes in Berlin, c. 530 B.C. Below: Fight in the ring, shoulder throw.
Bowl in London, c. 430 B.C.

Wrestler's grip in a battle with centaurs. Mixing bowl (Krater) in Florence, c. 460 B.C.

Runners. Above: Long distance runners underway on a crowded course. Panathenaic prize amphora in the Vatican, 5th century B.C. Below: Torch-light run to the altar. Attic Krater, 5th century B.C.

Armed runner at the starting point. Bronze statuette in Tübingen, Archaeol. Inst., c. 470 B.C.

Above: Girls in swimming pool. Amphora by the potter Andokides in Paris, c. 530 B.C. Below: Chariot race, quadrigae. Attic lekythos in San Francisco, c. 510 B.C.

Scenes from the Palaestra. Above: Boys cleaning themselves with strigilis (scraping iron). Interior picture of a bowl by the Euaion painter in the Vatican, c. 450 B.C. Below: Youths attending to their bodies, (foot massage, oiling). Mixing bowl by Euphronios in Berlin, c. 500 B.C.

Youth with pick and basket attending to running track. Picture inside bowl by the Panaitios painter in Brussels, c. 490 B.C.

Victorious youth at a javelin throwing contest on the podium. Inside picture of a bowl, c. 510 B.C.

172

Honoring the victor with bands and branches. Attic water jug (Hydria) in Munich, c. 510 B.C.

Victorious charioteer. Votive present for a victor of the Polyzalos at Gela. Original bronze by the sculptor Sotades from Thespiae in Delphi, c. 470 B.C.

Picture of Satyros, nine times victor in the Boxing Ring. Head of the bronze statue by Silanios in Olympia, c. 330 B.C.

Boy riding, holding whip and wearing spurs. Remainder of a group of riders. Bronze, Hellenistic period, in Athens, Nat. Mus.

Pankratiast fighting and using feet as well as fists. Bronze statue from the time of the Roman emperors in Paris, Louvre.

Boy playing with a wooden hoop. Attic marble relief in Athens, Nat. Mus., 4th century B.C.

Ball game with curved bats, a type of hockey, played in teams. Boys waiting for the ball. Relief from the base of a statue in Athens, Nat. Mus., c. 480 B.C.

Above: Boys at a ball game being carried on the shoulders of men. Amphora in London, end of the 6th century. Below: "Ephedrismos" a game of pick-a-back where the bearer, his eyes blindfolded, has to touch a stone. Jug in Berlin, c. 430 B.C.

Above: Girls on a swing. Two-handled goblet (Skyphos) by the painter of "Penelope" in Berlin, c. 470 B.C.

Right: Man and boy playing with a top. Interior picture of a bowl in the Robinson Collection, c. 480 B.C.

Above: Playing dice with knucklebones. Young girl. Roman copy of the 2nd century A.D. from a Hellenistic original in Berlin. Below: Kneeling boy in the position of a dice player. Bronze statuette in Berlin, c. 450 B.C.

Girl playing "Kottabos" with her feet. From an Apulian mixing bowl (Krater) in Genoa, early Hellenistic.

Donkey used as bait at a lion hunt. Ionian water jug (Hydria) from Caere in Berlin, c. 530 B.C.

Huntsman killing a wild boar with a sword in a rocky valley. Interior picture of a bowl in the Gallatin Collection, 5th century.

Young huntsman fully equipped with hound, probably Cephalus, the lover of Eos (Aurora), goddess of the dawn. Lekythos (oil vessel) by the "Pan-painter". Boston c. 480 B.C.

Above: Hunting the boar with spear and dogs; stag hunting with nets. Relief on a sarcophagus in Rome, Mus. Nuovo, 3rd century A.D. Below: Returning from the hunt with a captured bear. Relief on a sarcophagus in Rome, Palace of the Conservators, 2nd century A.D.

Return from the hunt. Relief on a sarcophagus in Pisa, 2nd century A.D.

Hound licking himself. Relief on an Etruscan terracotta urn in the Vatican, hellenistic.

Pottery. Above: Workmen in clay-pit. Corinthian terracotta tile (Pinax) from Pendeskufia by Acrocorinth. 1st half of 6th century B.C., in Berlin. Athena modelling a horse out of clay. Attic wine jug (Oinochoe) in Berlin, c. 470 B.C.

Brass-foundry. Above: Working the furnace and working on a statue of a boy. Below: Putting final touches to completed statue of a warrior supervised by the master-craftsman. Attic bowl in Berlin, c. 480 B.C.

Smith's workshop. Vulcan (Hephaestus) and his helpers, the Cyclopes, forging a suit of armour for Achilles. Votive relief in Rome, Palace of the Conservators, 2nd century A.D. time of Hadrian.

Painter of statues putting the colour on the completed figure of Hercules. Italian mixing bowl in New York, 4th century B.C.

Smith's workshop. Vulcan's helpers carrying out intricate work on the grieve for a leg. Pompeiian Mural, 1st century A.D.

Butcher's shop, cutting up, turning and frying meat on spits. Boeotic lid of a bowl, c. 500 B.C., in Adolphseck.

Cobbler's workroom. Shoes made to measure. Attic Pelike in Oxford, c. 470 B.C.

Woman buying oil in small quantities. Pelike in Adolphseck, c. 450 B.C.

Selling pigs. Pelike in Cambridge, c. 460 B.C.

Above: Stall and storage place. Roman relief in the Vatican from the time of the Emperors. Below: Artisans' workshops. Left: A cobbler at work. Right: Spinning room. On a sarcophagus from Ostia, in Rome, Mus. Naz.

Above: Purchasers at a clothier's. Relief from a tomb in Florence 1st century A.D. Below: Cutler with goods for sale and work table. Roman relief from a tomb, time of the Emperors.

Above: Transferring of goods from one ship to another. Mosaic in Ostia. 2nd century A.D.
Below: Porters. From the tomb of L. Calpurnius in Rome, Palazzo Massimi, 3rd century A.D.

A big machine for lifting heavy weights worked by means of a treadle wheel. Part of relief from the tomb of the Haterii, in the Lateran, 1st century A.D. Flavian.

Bakeries. Above: Corn mill and oven in Pompeii. Below: Corn mills in a house in Ostia.

Greek coins.

10 Drachmae – silver coin from Syracuse with the head of the Nymph of the Wells, Arethusa. After 400 B.C.

Northern Greek silver coin bearing the head of Zeus of Olympia by Pheidias. 4th century B.C.

Greek coins. Above: 4 Drachmae – silver coin from Athens. On the front the head of Athena, on the back an owl and inscription, c. 470 B.C. Below: 2 Drachmae – silver coin from Thasos. Front: satyr and nymph; back: squares. End of the 6th century.

Greek coins. Above: Silver coins from Myrina (Asia Minor) with head and statue of Apollo, Hellenistic. Below: Macedonian silver coin with the portrait of King Perseus (178–168 B.C.) and the eagle of Zeus within a wreath of spruce.

Roman money. Above: Gold coin with the head of the Emperor Hadrian (117–138). On the back: The Emperor on horseback at the Adlocution. Below: Aes Grave, 1 As, the oldest Roman money (bronze) bearing the head of Janus, time of the Republic.

Floor mosaic used as display signs in Ostia representing merchant ships in harbor. Above: The lighthouse at Ostia. Below: Display sign of the shipping firm of Karalis (Cagliari).

Above: Man carrying sack (saccarii) at the unloading of a ship. Relief in the cathedral at Salerno. Below: The harbor of Ostia. Relief in Rome, Palazzo Torlonia, c. 200 A.D.

Peasant carrying sacrificial calf to the temple. Marble statue. Votive present from Rhombos to Athena, Athens, Acropolis Museum, c. 570 B.C.

Above: Grape harvest. Two handled jug in Paris, 6th century B.C. Below: Men beating ripe olives from a tree. Attic Amphora in Berlin, c. 520–510 B.C.

Above: Wine press. Relief in Athens, Nat. Mus. Below: Peasant plowing with oxen in the presence of Athena (Minerva). Etruscan bronze group in Rome, Villa Giulia, 4th century B.C.

Above: Herd of cattle, five cows and one bull. The Euphronios bowl in Munich, c. 510 B.C.
Below: Shepherds with their herds, horses, cattle, sheep. A sarcophagus relief in Rome, Mus.
Naz., 3rd century A.D.

Fisherman's hut on an island in the river Nile. "Mosaic Barberini" from Palestrina (Praeneste) in Rome, Mus. Naz., 3rd century A.D. Below: A herd of goats and a rustic sanctuary. Mosaic from the Villa of Hadrian in Tivoli, in the Vatican, 2nd century A.D.

Lady with parasol driving in a carriage with two wheels. Etruscan tombstone in Bologna, 4th century B.C.

Driving in a four-wheeled carriage. Roman relief on a tombstone in Verona, time of the emperors.

Above: Roman carriage. Relief from Virunum, on the south elevation of the church in Maria Saal (Carinthia). Below: Quadrigae, triumphal carriage of Emperor Marcus Aurelius. Triumphal relief in Rome, Palace of the Conservators, 2nd century A.D.

Interior courtyards. Above: Greek peristyle house on Delos, Hellenistic. Below: Roman Atrium house in Pompeii, 1st century A.D.

Above: Large courtyard with colonnade (Porticus) at one time two storied; summer house and artificial pond within. Villa of Diomedes in Pompeii, 1st century A.D. Below: Arcade inside the "Casa delle Muse" in Ostia, 2nd century A.D., time of Hadrian.

Dining room (Triclinium) in a Pompeian house, 1st century A.D.

Domestic chapel (Lararium) in Pompeii, 1st century A.D.

Well ornamented with mosaic in the garden (Viridarium) of a
Pompeian house. 1st century A.D.

Greek gravel mosaic in a house in Olynthus: Bellerophon riding Pegasus and killing Chimaera, 4th century B.C.

Above: Floor mosaic in a house on Delos; two dolphins harnessed by Eros. 2nd century B.C. Below: The signature of the artist Hephaestion, mosaic from the royal palace of Pergamum. In Berlin, 2nd century B.C.

Above: Floor, peristyle in a house on Delos, 2nd century B.C. Below: Border on the Corinthian oecus of the "Casa del Labirinto" in Pompeii, 1st century A.D.

Watchdog on a chain. Floor mosaic from
Pompeii in Naples, 1st century A.D.

Skeleton; the inscription below reads: "Know thyself". From a house on the Via Appia. In Rome,
Mus. Naz., time of the Emperors.

Mural decoration from the house of Livia on the Palatine in Rome, so-called II style, about the birth of Christ.

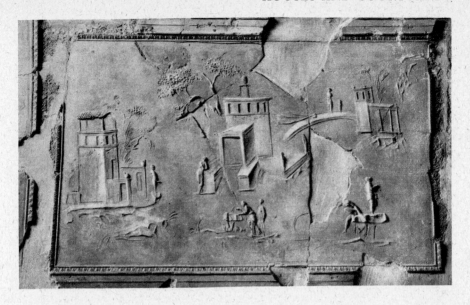

Frescoes. Above: Landscape, stucco relief. Rome, Mus. Naz., at the time of the birth of Christ. Below: Stucco relief from the Basilica Pl. 42, in Rome, 1st century A.D. A dioscuros abducting a Leukippide.

Above: Dressing the bride. Attic "Lutrophorus" in Athens, end of 5th century B.C. Below, left: Woman wearing a wreath of myrtle. Lekythos in Giessen, c. 440 B.C. Below, right: Young man lifting bride into carriage. "Lutrophorus" in Berlin, c. 430 B.C.

Married couples. Above: Married couple in reclining position about to eat. Etruscan terra cotta sarcophagus from Caere in Rome, Villa Giulia, c. 530 B. C. Below: Roman couple in conversation. Relief from a sarcophagus lid in Rome, Capitol Museum, 2nd century A.D.

223

Old nurse holding a child. Terra cotta statuette in New York, Hellenistic.

Woman carrying a naked child in her arms. Terra cotta statuette in Berlin, 2nd century B.C.

Left: Girl with a little dog. Bronze statuette in New York, Hellenistic. Right: Mother standing before her little boy in his chair. Lekythos in Berlin, c. 460 B.C.

Parents and children going for a drive (boy with a goose, boy with a "scooter"). Relief from a child's sarcophagus in Rome, time of the Emperors.

Boy sitting on comfortable armchair. Interior picture of the Duris bowl, in New York, c. 500 B.C.

Danae, in anticipation of the golden shower, seated on a couch (Kline) with cushion and coverlet. Water jug (Hydria) in Adolphseck, 5th century B.C.

Women at home. Left: A girl carrying a chest. Attic water jug in Berlin, c. 450 B.C. Below: Doctor on a folding chair with backrest seated in front of his medicine chest. Sarcophagus relief in Rome, 3rd century A.D.

Youth drawing water from a well. Interior picture of a bowl in London about 480 B.C.

Woman pumping water from a well. Mixing bowl (Krater) in Tübingen, 5th century B.C.

Girl by a natural well in the form of a lion's head.
Lekythos in Paris, c. 500 B.C.

Girl inside a well house accosted by a man.
Water jug in Berlin, early 5th century B.C.

Girl at a large wash basin. Mixing bowl in Bari, c. 520 B.C.

Youth with scraper standing by a wash basin; right, a boy cleaning his master's sandals. Jug (pelike) in Berlin, c. 490 B.C.

Left: Girl (Aphrodite?) being attended by Eros while washing her hair. So-called Acorn lekythos by Meidias in Berlin, c. 400 B.C.

Right: Bronze mirror with the handle shaped like the figure of a girl, in Copenhagen, 5th century.

Woman with a mirror in her hand attending to her toilet. Krater in Athens, 4th century B.C.

Two women at their toilet. Engraving on Greek mirror in New York, 4th century B.C.

Girls wearing long-sleeved garment (Chiton) with short coat (Himation). From the Amphora by Euthymides in Munich, c. 510 B.C.

Left: Girl tying girdle beneath the folds of her dress. Hydria in Berlin, c. 460 B.C. Right: Girl wearing diaphanous gown. Interior picture of an Etruscan bowl from Chiusi, in Berlin, 4th century B.C.

Young girl with circular hat and heart-shaped fan wearing a big cloak and undergarment. Terra cotta statuette from Tanagra in Berlin, c. 320 B.C.

Roman couple, man wearing tunic and toga made of a small amount of cloth, early period, the woman wearing a Greek garment. Compare Pl. 234, Relief on a tomb in Rome, Museo Nuovo, time of the Roman Emperors (early).

Roman wearing an ample toga of the late period attending a sacrifice. Statue of Pentelian marble in the Vatian, 2nd half of the 1st century A.D.

Greek female coiffure with center parting, double band in front and loose knot at the back. Copy of a Greek original from the 4th century B.C., in Berlin.

Roman coiffures. Young girl with turned under hair on forehead and large nest-like knot at the back. Marble bust in Rome, Mus. Naz., Augustan age.

Roman coiffures. Roman woman wearing wig dressed in a high curly style, own hair at the back worn in twisted knot. Marble bust in Rome, Palazzo Rospigliosi, c. 80 A.D.

Woman with plaited hair-crown. Mummy from Egypt, in Berlin, 2nd century A.D.

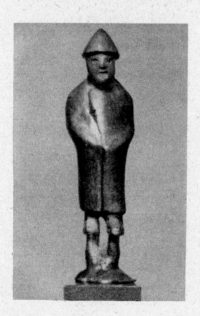 

Above: Young shepherd with fur cap. From the bell Krater by the Pan painter in Boston, c. 470 B.C. Below: Shepherds with hat and cap. Bronze statuettes from Arcadia in Berlin, c. 500 B.C.

Girl (Maenad attacked by a Satyr) wearing a cap. From the Amphora by the Cleophrades painter in Munich, about 500 B.C.

Left: The beautiful Leagros on horseback wearing a dainty hat. Interior picture of a bowl by Euphronius in Munich, c. 510 B.C.

Girl putting on hair ribbon. From an Attic vase painting in Brunswick, c. 450 B.C.

Girl with hair band which is knotted on forehead. Bride from the West Pediment of the Temple of Zeus, Olympia, c. 460 B.C.

Sacrificial boy attendants (Camilli) wearing short, sleeveless tunics. One boy holding sacrificial basket, the other carrying half-open parasol. Relief on a funeral altar in Rome, Mus. Naz., early part of 1st century A.D., time of Claudius.

Girl tying her sandal. Interior picture of a bowl in Berlin, c. 520 B.C.

Below: Roman sandal with elaborate straps. From the relief on Pl. 145 in Rome, Capitol Museum,
c. 80 A.D.

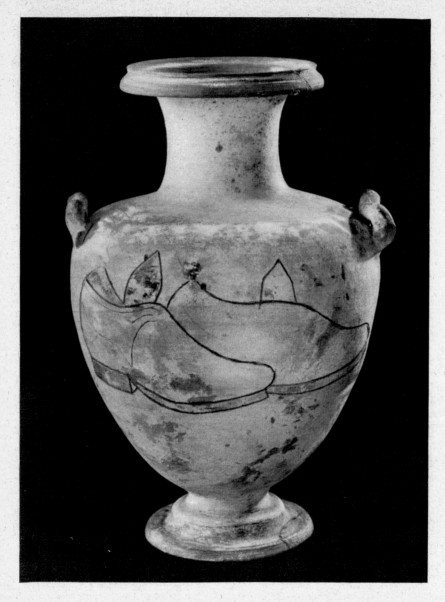

A pair of woman's leather shoes. Drawing on a water jug (Hydria) painted white, in Tübingen, Hellenistic.

Young woman with tattooed arms and legs. Thracian woman carrying arms, from an Attic mixing bowl (Krater) by the Pan painter, in Munich, c. 470 B.C.

Above: Chamber music in the women's quarters. Woman playing lyre. Mixing bowl in Giessen, c. 450–440 B.C. Below: Boys and men making music and singing. Mixing bowl by Phintias, in Munich, c. 510 B.C.

Enthusiastic cithara player and man listening.
Picture on a vase in Boston, c. 500 B.C.

Muse on the Helicon playing the lyre. From a mixing bowl with a white background in the Vatican, c. 440 B.C.

The muse Terpsichore playing the harp. From an Attic Amphora by the Peleus Painter in London, c. 450–440 B.C.

Above: Young teacher and student with lyre. Attic jug in London, c. 440 B.C. Below: Blowing the trumpet. Amazons at the onset of battle. Water jug (Hydria) by Hypsis in Munich, c. 500 B.C.

Boy with double flute and mouth covered by a band. From an Amphora by the Cleophrades painter in London, c. 500 B.C.

Young flute player and man singing at a symposium. Interior picture of a bowl by Duris, in Munich, c. 480 B.C.

Dancing girl and woman playing the flute beating time with her foot. "Italiotic" Krater in Berlin, c. 450 B.C.

Tuba player from one of Marcus Aurelius'
Triumphal Reliefs (169–180 A.D.), in Rome,
Capitol Museum.

Below: Fife player. Relief from an Etruscan
funeral urn in the Volumnier grave near Perugia,
c. 100 B.C.

Girl with long double flute of the Roman period. Muse on a sarcophagus with columns in Rome, Mus. Naz., c. 300 A.D.

Young men dancing to the accompaniment of the flute. Boeotian basin from the Cabiri sanctuary near Thebes in Berlin, 4th century B.C.

Man dancing grotesque dance. Ionic beaker in Berlin, after 550 B.C.

Dancing girl with castanets (Crotala).
Interior picture of a bowl in Cambridge (Mass.), c. 520 B.C.

Girl dancing and banging tambourine (Tympanum). Fragment in Rome, c. 400 B.C.

Greek dancer on her toes executing a pirouette. Attic relief in Berlin. End of the 5th century B.C.

Ecstatic dancer, raving Maenad with a mangled animal. Neo-Attic relief in Rome, Capitol Mus., 1st century A.D.

Dancer (Maenad) with tambourine (Tympanum). Picture by the Cleophon painter in Munich, c. 430 B.C.

Banquet (Symposium) men drinking on couch.
Pictures on an Attic bowl in the Vatican, 500 to
490 B.C.

Man feasting on couch (Kline) with dining table in front of him. Achilles, visited by Priam (Hector's corpse on the floor) giving instructions to cupbearer. Picture on a beaker by the Brygos painter in Vienna, c. 490 B.C.

Cupbearer with wine sieve and long ladle. Part of picture on opposite page.

Woman playing Kottaboss (a love oracle) watched by the cupbearer. Jug in Berlin, c. 440 B.C.

Youth at a symposium, standing before him a girl (Hetaera) gathering her skirt as if to dance. Interior picture of a bowl by the Brygos painter, in London, c. 490 B.C.

After effects of over-feasting. Interior picture of the bowl, shown on Pl. 261, in the Vatican, about 500–490 B.C.

Right: Dancing youth (Komastes) with a wine tube. Interior picture of a bowl by the Euergides painter in Athens, Nat. Mus., c. 520–510 B.C.

Below: Youth ladling wine out of a jug, also a male dancer (Komastes). Picture on a bowl in Vienna, c. 520 B.C.

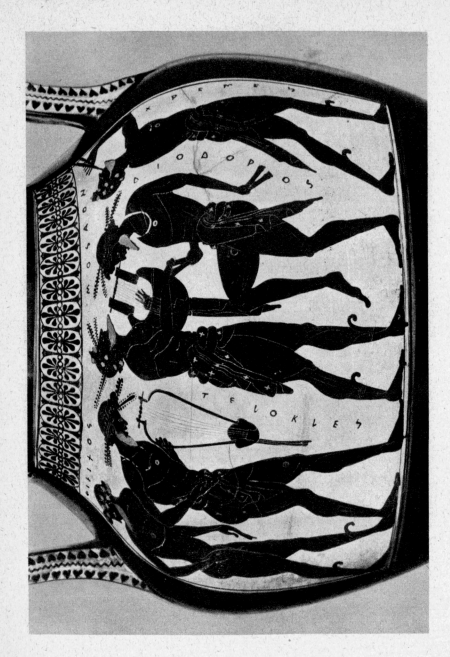

Dancing and singing men returning from a symposium. Amphora in Munich, c. 500 B.C.

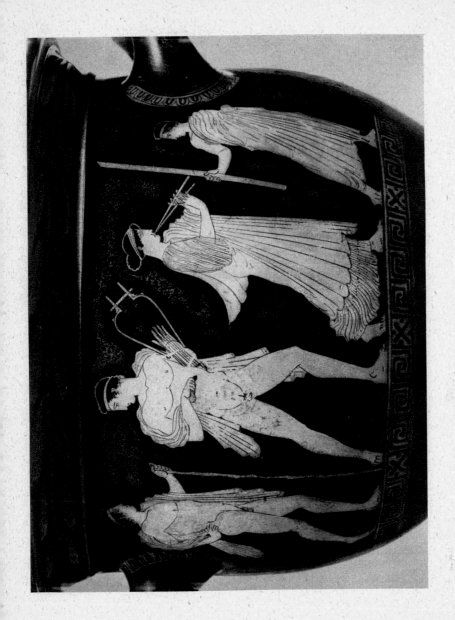

Return at night from a symposium. Picture on a Krater in Detroit (Michigan), c. 430 B.C.

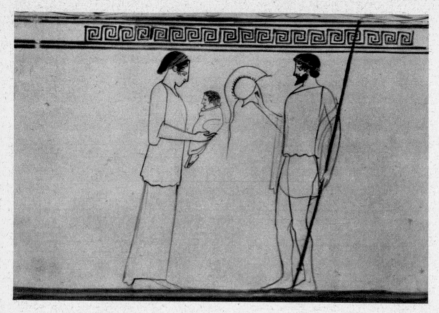

Woman holding suckling baby at the departure of the man into battle. Oil can (lekythos) with a white background, in Berlin, c. 460 B.C.

Woman raising a child up to a bunch of grapes. "Choen" jug in Erlangen, end of 5th century B.C.

Grandmother with her grandchild. Tombstone of
Ampharete in Athens, Kerameikos Mus., c. 410 B.C.

Mourning child. Fragment from a tomb in Athens,
Nat. Mus. c. 350 B.C.

Little boy holding on to a goose trying to escape. Marble group after a bronze original by Boethus of Carthage in Munich, 3rd century B.C.

Sleeping child wearing pointed cap and carrying lantern. Roman copy after a Hellenistic original in Rome, Mus. Naz.

Girl with pigeon. Marble figure in Rome, Capitol Mus., Roman copy from a Hellenistic original of the 2nd century B.C.

Young girl. Greek original from Antium in Rome,
Mus. Naz., 3rd century B.C.

Ephebus. Head from a tombstone from Sunion in
Athens, Nat. Mus., 480 B.C.

Sitting Ephebus. Terra cotta statuette in Adolphseck, 3rd century B.C.

Girl sitting. Marble statue in Rome, Palace of the
Conservators, 3rd century.

Young woman bidding her father farewell. Attic funeral Lekythos in Munich, c. 320 B.C.

Young girl at sacrifice. Marble statue from Antium, Rome, Mus. Naz., 3rd century B.C.

Young woman bringing pigeon to be sacrificed. Greek tombstone from the Esquiline in Rome, Palace of the Conservators, c. 470 B.C.

Youth and small attendant with cleaning utensils. Marble stele in the Vatican, c. 450 B.C.

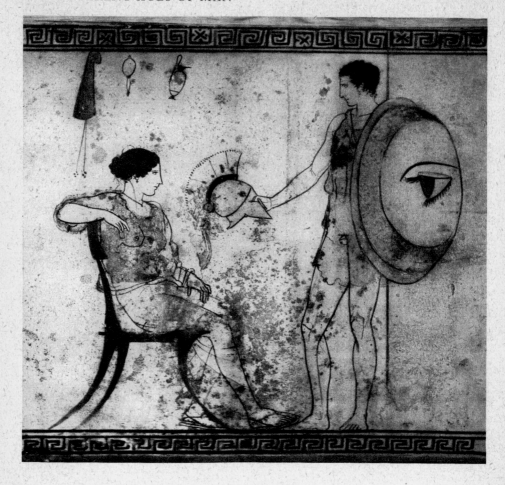

Young warrior parting from his wife. White Lekythos by the Achilles Painter in Athens, c. 450 B.C.

Young woman having her hair combed. Fragment
in Rome, c. 420 B.C.

Young veiled woman with scent bottle. Mural
in Rome, Mus. Naz., 1st century A.D.

Hector's farewell from his ancient father Priam
(above) and his mother Hecuba. Amphora by the
Hector Painter in the Vatican, c. 450 B.C.

Old man. From an Attic tombstone in Athens, Nat. Mus., c. 350 B.C.

Very old woman, the "intoxicated old woman" with a bottle of wine (Lagynos). In Munich, Glyptothek, c. 250 B.C.

Old market-woman. Marble statue in New York, c. 100 B.C.

Above left: Baldheaded old man. Etruscan terra cotta head in Orvieto, end of 5th century. Above right: Old man, perhaps a poet. Bronze head in Naples. Hellenistic. Below: Old market-woman crying out her wares. Marble head in Dresden. Albertinum, 1st century B.C.

Above: Old hunchbacked beggar. Bronze statuette from Alexandria in Berlin, c. 100 B.C. Below: Asclepius, the divine healer, healing a sick person. Votive relief in Athens, 4th century B.C.

At the doctor's. Above: Dwarf. Below: A young doctor letting blood. Round oil vessel (Aryballos) in Paris, "School of Makron", c. 480 B. C.

Men at a funeral procession. Painted terra cotta tile (Pinax) by Lydos in Athens, c. 550 B.C.

Above: Gathering of women at the mourning of the deceased. Painted terra cotta tile by Exekias in Berlin, c. 540 B.C. Below: Lying in state of the deceased (Prothesis) and mourning. Pinax in Paris, c. 540 B.C.

Above: Terra cotta coffin in the shape of a kline with a couple seated upon it. From Caere in Rome, Villa Giulia, Etruscan, c. 530 B.C. Below: Wailing at the lying in state of the corpse (Expositio). Urn for ashes in Rome, Mus. Naz., c. 200 A.D.

Above: Circular tomb (Soros) for those fallen in the battle of Marathon, 490 B.C. Below: Bricked in circular tomb in Lindos, so-called tomb of Kleobulus.

The lion of Chaeronea. Monument for the Thebans who fell in battle, 338 B.C., against Philip of Macedon.

Large area of tombs in the cemetery at Eridanus in Athens, 4th century B.C.

Above: Etruscan circular tombs from the city of tombs at Caere (Cerveteri). Below: Tombs on both sides of the road, Via Appia. Tombs date from Roman times.

Above: Tomb of Caecilia Metella on the Via Appia, Rome, Augustan period. Below: The mausoleum of Augustus, entrance. In Rome, erected 27 B.C.

The Sepulcher of the Julii in St. Remy, late Republic.

Sepulcher of the rich baker Eurisaces in Rome in front of the Porta Maggiore, end of the 1st century B.C.

Naked Ephebus ("Apollo Strangford"). In London, about 500 B.C.

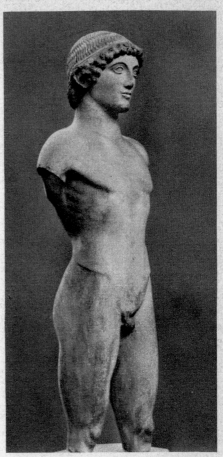

Young servant from a tomb in Tarento, Berlin, c. 300 B.C.

Lion guarding a tomb. Marble from Miletus in Berlin, 4th century B.C.

Mourning servant girls. Figures from an Attic tomb in Berlin, 4th century B.C.

Narrow tombstone of a young girl "Stele Giustiniani". In Berlin, work from one of the Greek islands, c. 460 B.C.

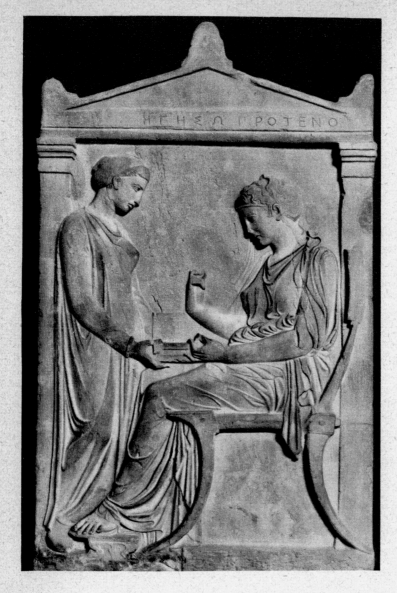

Broad tombstone in the shape of a flat aedicula. Monument of Hegeso from the cemetery on the Eridanus in Athens, c. 410 B.C.

Tomb of a Roman married couple. In front of the Porta Maggiore, Rome, c. 30 B.C.

Above: Tombstone of Athenian, in Berlin, late Hellenistic. Below: Roman family tomb ornamented with busts of the deceased. In Rome, Mus. Naz., 1st century A.D.

The deceased sitting at the base of her tombstone. Lekythos from Athens, in Berlin, c. 450 B.C.

Above: Women with sacrificial utensils on their way to the grave. White lekythos in Athens, c. 460 B.C. Below: Sacrifice at the grave. Attic beaker (Skyphos) in Copenhagen, c. 400 B.C.

Oath by the tomb. Orestes, Electra and Pylades at the tomb of Agamemnon. Terra cotta relief from Melos in Berlin, c. 430 B.C.

Roman tomb shaped like an altar on the street, bordered by tombs, outside the Gate of Herculaneum at Pompeii, 1st century A.D.